A DIVIDED UNION?
THE USA 1945–1970

GCSE Modern World History for Edexcel

Steve Waugh
John Wright

This material has been endorsed by Edexcel and offers high quality support for the delivery of Edexcel qualifications. Edexcel endorsement does not mean that this material is essential to achieve any Edexcel qualification, nor does it mean that this is the only suitable material available to support any Edexcel qualification. No endorsed material will be used verbatim in setting any Edexcel examination and any resource lists produced by Edexcel shall include this and other appropriate texts. While this material has been through an Edexcel quality assurance process, all responsibility for the content remains with the publisher. Copies of official specifications for all Edexcel qualifications may be found on the Edexcel website – www.edexcel.org.uk.

The Publishers would like to thank the following for permission to reproduce copyright material:

Photo credits
p. 4 Library of Congress (LC-USZ62-36154); **p. 5** © Corbis; **p. 9** *l* Catechetical Guild; **p. 9** *r* Getty Images; **p. 10** The Granger Collection/Topfoto; **p. 12, 13** *both*, **14, 15** © Bettmann/Corbis; **p. 17** © 1954 by the Washington Post; renewed by Herblock/Library of Congress (LC-USZ62-126910); **p. 18** *t* © Corbis/Bettmann; **p. 18** *b* © 20th Century Fox/The Kobal Collection; **p. 21** © Picture History/Library of Congress (LC-USZ62-75138); **p. 22** © Allied Artists/The Kobal Collection; **p. 23** Library of Congress (LC-USZ62-36154); **p. 24** © 1960 by The Washington Post Co.; renewed by Herblock/Library of Congress (LC-USZ62-127075); **p. 25** *l* Getty Images; **p. 25** *r* AP/Wide World Photos; **p. 26** © Bettmann/Corbis; **p. 27** Library of Congress (LC-USW3-034282); **p. 28** *l* © Bettmann/Corbis; **p. 28** *r* © Corbis; **p. 30** © Bettmann/Corbis; **p. 31** Library of Congress (LC-USZ62-111236); **p. 32** *t* Library of Congress (LC-U9- 2908-15); **p. 32** *b* Library of Congress; **p. 33** © Bettmann/Corbis; **p. 35** Holt Labor Library; **p. 36** Montgomery County Archives; **p. 38** *both* Time & Life Pictures/Getty Images; **p. 39** The Granger Collection/Topfoto; **p. 40, 41** Time & Life Pictures/Getty Images; **p. 44** © Bettmann/Corbis; **p. 45** Library of Congress (LC-USZ62-116815); **p. 47** © Jack Moebes/Corbis; **p. 48** © David J. & Janice L. Frent Collection/Corbis; **p. 50** *both* © Bettmann/Corbis; **p. 52** Time & Life Pictures/Getty Images; **p. 53** Library of Congress (LC-USZ62-133063); **p. 54** Time & Life Pictures/Getty Images; **p. 56** AP/Wide World Photos; **p. 57** © Bettmann/Corbis; **p. 58** *t* Library of Congress (LC-USZ62-133369); **58** *b* © Hulton-Deutsch Collection/Corbis; **p. 62** © Bettmann/Corbis; **p. 64** John F. Kennedy Presidential Library and Museum; **p. 65** © Flip Schulke/Corbis; **p. 66** Associated Press; **p. 67** Getty Images; **p. 69, 71, 76, 78** *both* © Bettmann/Corbis; **p. 79** © Flip Schulke/Corbis; **p. 80** *l* © Bettmann/Corbis; **p. 80** *r* Topfoto; **p. 81** © Ted Streshinsky/Corbis; **p. 82** © David J. & Janice L. Frent Collection/Corbis; p. 84 l Topfoto; **p. 85** © Jerry Schatzberg/Corbis; **p. 86** both © Bettmann/Corbis; **p. 87** © Jerry Schatzberg/Corbis; **p. 88** © Bettmann/Corbis; **p. 89, 90** Berkeley Digital Library; **p. 91, 93** © Bettmann/Corbis; **p. 94** © Harvey L. Silver/Corbis; **p. 95** Getty Images; **p. 96** © Henry Diltz/Corbis; **p. 97** Getty Images; **p. 99** Time & Life Pictures/Getty Images; **p. 102** © Corbis; **p. 103** Popperfoto.com; **p. 104** © Bettmann/Corbis; *p. 108 l* AP/Wide World Photos; **p. 108** *r* © Bettmann/Corbis; **p. 110** *t* both AP/Wide World Photos; **p. 110** *bl* © Bettmann/Corbis; **p. 110** *br* Getty Images; **p. 111** © Bettmann/Corbis; **p. 112** © JP Laffont/Sygma/Corbis.

Artwork
p. 14, 16, 43, 61, 100, 107 Big Blu Ltd; p. 49 Stefan Chabluk

Acknowledgements
p. 3 Edexcel Limited, specification booklet for the new specifications History A The Making of the Modern World, pp. 114–18; **p. 8, 9** *all* S. Waugh and J. Wright, *Peace and War: International Relations 1943–91*, Hodder, 2009; **p. 10** T. Lancaster and D. Peaple, *The Modern World*, Causeway, 1996; **p. 21** W. Manchester, *The Glory and the Dream*, 1974; **p. 27** D. Davis, *Mr Black Labour*, 1972; **p. 30** R. Field, *Civil Rights in America 1865–1980*, Cambridge University Press, 2002; **p. 34** 'Oxford Town' Copyright ©1963; renewed 1991 Special Rider Music. All rights reserved. International copyright secured. Reprinted by permission; **p. 39** Martin Luther King, *Stride Toward Freedom*, 1958; **p. 44** V. Sanders, *Race Relations in the USA since 1900*, Hodder and Stoughton, 2000; **p. 50** James Zwerg in an interview of 1999, quoted on www.pbs.org/wgbh/peoplescentury/; **p. 51** *b* V. Harding, 'The Other American Revolution', quoted in M. Marable, *Race, Reform and Rebellion*, University Press of Mississippi, 1991; **p. 55** 'Only a Pawn in Their Game' Copyright ©1963; renewed 1991 Special Rider Music. All rights reserved. International copyright secured. Reprinted by permission; **p. 62** *l* F. Powledge, *Free at Last?*, Little Brown, 1991; **p. 62** *r* M. Marable, *Race, Reform and Rebellion*, University Press of Mississippi, 1991; **p. 76** From Malcolm X's autobiography, quoted in M. Marable, *Race, Reform and Rebellion*, University Press of Mississippi, 1991; **p. 81, 82** *both* Reprinted on Spartacus Educational at www.spartacus.schoolnet.co.uk/USAcivilrights.htm; **p. 85** 'Blowin' in the Wind' Copyright ©1963; renewed 1991 Special Rider Music. All rights reserved. International copyright secured. Reprinted by permission; **p. 98** *t* A. Huber, C. Lemieux and M. Hollis, *The Hippie Generation*, 2004; **p. 98** *tm* N. Smith, *The USA, 1917–80*, Oxford University Press, 1996; **p. 98** *bm* C. Appy, *Vietnam*, Ebury, 2003; **p. 101** Statistics from N. Smith, *The USA, 1917–80*, Oxford University Press, 1996; **p. 105** B. Friedan, *The Feminine Mystique*, 1963; **p. 107** *b* Statistics from N. Smith, *The USA, 1917–80*, Oxford University Press, 1996; **p. 111** *tl* N. Smith, *The USA, 1917–80*, Oxford University Press, 1996; **p. 111** *br* B. Friedan, *The Feminine Mystique*, 1963; **p. 112** B. Walsh, *Modern World*, Murray, 1996.

Every effort has been made to trace all copyright holders, but if any have been inadvertently overlooked the Publishers will be pleased to make the necessary arrangements at the first opportunity.

Although every effort has been made to ensure that website addresses are correct at time of going to press, Hodder Education cannot be held responsible for the content of any website mentioned in this book. It is sometimes possible to find a relocated web page by typing in the address of the home page for a website in the URL window of your browser.

Orders: please contact Bookpoint Ltd, 130 Milton Park, Abingdon, Oxon OX14 4SB. Telephone: (44) 01235 827720. Fax: (44) 01235 400454. Lines are open 9.00 – 5.00, Monday to Saturday, with a 24-hour message answering service. Visit our website at www.hoddereducation.co.uk.

Introduction

About the course

During this course you must study four units:

- **Unit 1** Peace and War: International Relations 1900–1991
- **Unit 2** Modern World Depth Study
- **Unit 3** Modern World Source Enquiry
- **Unit 4** Representations of History.

These units are assessed through three examination papers and one controlled assessment:

- In Unit 1 you have one hour and 15 minutes to answer questions on three different sections from International Relations 1900–1991.
- In Unit 2 you have one hour and 15 minutes to answer questions on a Modern World Depth Study.
- In Unit 3 you have one hour and 15 minutes to answer source questions on one Modern World Source Enquiry topic.
- In the controlled assessment you have to complete a task under controlled conditions in the classroom (Unit 4).

About the book

This book has been written to support option 3c 'A divided union? The USA 1945–70' in Unit 3. It covers the key developments in the USA from 1945 to 1970. The book is divided into four key topics, each with three chapters:

- **Key Topic 1** examines the impact of the Cold War on the USA, the development of the Red Scare and the impact of McCarthyism.
- **Key Topic 2** explains the progress of the civil rights movement in education and the support for segregation, examines the causes and results of the Montgomery Bus Boycott, and looks at the leadership and methods of Martin Luther King in the years 1958–62.

- **Key Topic 3** examines the impact of the peace marches of 1963, the civil rights legislation of the mid-1960s, and the importance of Malcolm X and Black Power.
- **Key Topic 4** looks at other protest movements in the 1960s and explains the reasons for student protest, the key features of the student protest movement, and the reasons for and activities of the women's movement.

Each chapter in this book:

- Contains activities – some develop the historical skills you will need, others are exam-style questions that give you the opportunity to practise exam skills. The exam-style questions are highlighted in blue.
- Gives step-by-step guidance, model answers and advice on how to answer particular question types in Unit 3.
- Highlights glossary terms in bold the first time they appear in each key topic.

About Unit 3

Unit 3 is a test of:

- The ability to answer a range of source questions.
- Knowledge and understanding of the key developments in the USA in the years 1945–70.

Source questions

The exam paper will include five or six sources, including:

- Written sources, such as extracts from diaries, speeches, letters, poems, songs, biographies, autobiographies, memoirs, newspapers, modern history textbooks, the views of historians.
- Illustrations, such as photographs, posters, cartoons or paintings.

Contents

Below is a set of specimen questions (without the sources). You will be given step-by-step guidance throughout the book on how best to approach and answer these types of questions.

This is a **source interpretation** question, asking you to explain the purpose of the source – why it was produced. This question may be phrased as:
- What was the purpose of this photograph?
- Why was this photograph published?

This is an **inference** question. You have to get a message or messages from the source.

This is a **cross-referencing** question. It is asking you to compare the views of the three sources and explain whether or not they support the view given in the question. It can also be phrased as:
- How far do Sources A, B and C agree about the events at Little Rock?
- Do Sources A and B support the views of Source C about the events at Little Rock?

This is a **utility** question. It is asking you to decide how useful each source is. This could also be a **reliability** question, where you must decide how reliable each source is.

This is a **hypothesis testing** question. It is asking you to use the sources and your own knowledge to discuss a view and test a hypothesis.

UNIT 3   EXAM

1   Study Source A. What can you learn from Source A about events at Little Rock High School in 1957?

(6 marks)

2   Study Source C and use your own knowledge. Why was the photograph published so widely in the USA? Use details from the photograph and your own knowledge to explain the answer.

(8 marks)

3   Study Sources A, B and C and use your own knowledge. Do these sources support the view that the events at Little Rock in 1957 were carried out peacefully? Explain your answer.

(10 marks)

4   Study Sources D and E. Using the sources and your own knowledge, how useful are Sources D and E as evidence of the impact of the Montgomery Bus Boycott? Explain your answer.

(10 marks)

5   Study all the sources and use your own knowledge. 'The Montgomery Bus Boycott was the main reason for progress in civil rights for black Americans in the years 1945–60'. How far do the sources in this paper support this statement? Use the sources and your own knowledge to explain your answer.

(16 marks)

(Total 50 marks)

Key Topic 1: McCarthyism and the Red Scare

YEAH — SO HELP ME GOD!

LOYALTY OATH

Source A: **A cartoon of 1947 showing a person taking a loyalty oath**

Task

What can you learn from Source A about attitudes to those who were taking loyalty oaths? (For guidance on answering this type of question, see page 16.)

This key topic examines the fear of **communism** that developed in the USA in the years after 1945 and became known as the Red Scare. This fear of communism dated back to the **Bolshevik (communist) Revolution** of October 1917 in Russia. However, this fear intensified in the years after 1945 as the influence of the Soviet Union spread into Eastern Europe. The Truman Doctrine, Marshall Plan, Berlin Airlift, Hollywood Ten, the Rosenbergs and the Alger Hiss case were clear examples to the US authorities that the Soviet Union and the spread of communism had to be thwarted at all costs. The growing fear of communism was intensified by the actions of Joseph McCarthy.

Each chapter explains a key issue and examines important lines of enquiry as outlined below:

Chapter 1 The impact of the Cold War (pages 5–10)
- Why was there a fear of communism?

Chapter 2 The development of the Red Scare (pages 11–16)
- Why did events in the USA, 1945–50, increase the fear of communism?
- What was the importance of the Hiss and Rosenberg cases?

Chapter 3 The impact of McCarthyism (pages 17–23)
- Why was McCarthy able to win support?
- Why did McCarthyism fade away?
- What were the effects of McCarthyism?

1 The impact of the Cold War

MARSHALL PLAN DELAY

WESTERN EUROPE

Source A: A cartoon from 1948 showing Russia as a bear threatening Western Europe

Task

Study Source A and use your own knowledge. Why were cartoons like this published so widely in the USA? Use details from the cartoon and your own knowledge to explain the answer.
(For guidance on answering this type of question, see page 23.)

The fear of communism developed in the USA in the years after the Bolshevik Revolution of 1917 in Russia. Although the USA and the Soviet Union were allies during the Second World War, American distrust of communism continued. In the years after 1945, a Cold War developed between the USA and the Soviet Union. This led to an increase in fear and hatred of communism by most Americans. Communists, or those thought to have communist sympathies, faced great intolerance and the eventual loss of their political and other rights. 'Better dead than Red' became a popular slogan.

This chapter will answer the following question:

• Why was there a fear of communism?

Examination skills

In this chapter you will be given the opportunity to answer some of the question types from Unit 3.

Source A: **A cartoon published in the USA in 1919 entitled 'Come on!' (The American Legion was a patriotic organisation formed in 1919.)**

In Russia in October 1917, the Bolshevik Party seized power and overthrew the Provisional Government. This was known as the Bolshevik Revolution. After a civil war that lasted almost four years, opponents were defeated and the **Bolsheviks**, led by Lenin, began to set up a **communist** state.

Shortly after the Bolshevik Revolution, a wave of violent anti-communism spread across the USA. The communist views held by Lenin and the Bolsheviks were despised by many US citizens. The ideas were completely against **capitalism** – the system on which the USA had flourished in the nineteenth and early twentieth centuries. Any attempt to spread communism into the USA was resisted wholeheartedly.

The '**Red Scare**' was the fear of the spread of communism to the USA by immigrants from Eastern Europe. The Red Scare of 1919 and 1920 in the USA was whipped up by the press and public officials. President Wilson's **attorney general**, A. Mitchell Palmer, tried to clear out people he thought were communists – some Russian immigrants were sent back to their country of origin, thousands were arrested and, by the summer of 1920, it was felt that the spread of Bolshevism had been halted.

The hatred and fear of communism did not disappear completely. The United States did not recognise the government of the Union of Soviet Socialist Republics (**USSR**) until 1933. There was still a concern in the USA that the USSR wanted to destroy capitalism, and this seemed to be borne out when the Soviet Union invaded Poland in 1939 and went to war against Finland later that year.

	Communism	Capitalism
Politics	Only one political party – the Communist Party. No choice. People unable to change their government.	Several parties – voters have choice and can change their government.
Economy	No private industry or businesses. No private profit. All industry and businesses owned by the state for the benefit of everyone.	Most industry and businesses privately owned.
Beliefs	Everyone equal. Belief in world revolution – that is, encouraging communism in other countries. Censorship of the media.	Some people will be wealthier than others. Spread influence to other countries to encourage trade and investment. Very little censorship of the media.

The differences between communism and capitalism.

The Second World War

The USA and USSR were thrown together as allies in 1941, after the USA entered the Second World War following the Japanese attack on Pearl Harbor – yet the alliance remained uneasy and cautious. The leader of the USSR, Joseph Stalin, distrusted President Roosevelt and the USA because there seemed to be an unwillingness to open the second front in Europe against Hitler.

The events of 1945

At the Yalta Conference in February 1945, the USA and USSR were able to make some agreements about their approach to the post-war world. However, Roosevelt and Stalin could not agree fully on the fate of Germany, nor could Roosevelt persuade Stalin to remove Soviet troops from Eastern Europe. Between Yalta and Roosevelt's death in April 1945, communist governments were set up in Soviet-held territories. Stalin thus broke the promises made at Yalta that he would allow free elections in Eastern Europe.

Harry Truman, the new president, did not think that the USSR could be trusted, and his advisers urged him 'to get tough' with Stalin. At the Potsdam Conference in July 1945, Truman knew that the atomic bomb had been successfully tested and, in the words of Churchill, 'he generally bossed the whole meeting'. Truman did not feel that the alliance with the Soviet Union was now so important.

At the start of the conference, Truman informed Stalin about the testing of the atomic bomb. The Soviet leader was furious that he had not been consulted beforehand. The USA was confident that it would take the Soviet Union at least ten years to develop its own atomic bomb. Stalin could not wait that long, and the Soviet atomic research programme was transformed in 1945. Scientists' pay was trebled and by 1949 there was a team of half a million scientists working on the atomic programme. The USA was shocked when, in 1949, a US plane carrying scientific instruments found evidence of the first successful Soviet atomic test.

Tasks

1. *Study Source A and use your own knowledge. Why was this cartoon published? Use details from the cartoon and your own knowledge to explain the answer. (For guidance on answering this type of question, see page 23.)*

2. *Devise a suitable caption for the cartoon to show its message.*

Soviet expansion

Truman and many Americans were alarmed by Soviet expansion in Eastern Europe in the years 1945 to 1949. The map on this page shows the extent of Soviet expansion in these years.

Towards the end of the Second World War, Soviet troops had liberated country after country in Eastern Europe from Nazi occupation. However, instead of withdrawing his troops after the war, Stalin left them there. In 1947 **Cominform** (Communist Information Bureau) was set up to bring all European communist parties more firmly under Soviet control. By 1949, Hungary, Romania, Bulgaria, Poland and Czechoslovakia had become one-party communist states controlled by the Soviet Union. For example, in 1948, the Soviet Union prevented the development of democracy in Czechoslovakia by ensuring the Czech Communist Party was able to take control of the government.

The USA was convinced that Stalin's aim was to expand communism throughout Europe. Stalin, on the other hand, saw these countries in Eastern Europe as a buffer for the Soviet Union against possible future invasion from the West. Truman wanted to 'contain Russian expansive tendencies'. In March 1946, Churchill talked of an '**iron curtain**' separating the West and East in Europe – there seemed to be clear hostility between the former allies.

Map showing the countries in Eastern Europe under Soviet control by 1949.

Key
- Soviet gains 1939–40
- Soviet gains after 1945

Source B: Clement Attlee in 1960, recalling the Potsdam Conference of July 1945

The Russians had shown themselves even more difficult than anyone expected. After Potsdam, one couldn't be very hopeful any longer. It was quite obvious they were going to be troublesome. The war had left them holding positions far into Europe, much too far. I had no doubt they intended to use them.

Source C: George Kennan was a US official in Moscow. In 1946 he wrote a long telegram to President Truman, warning him about Soviet expansion.

It is clear that the United States cannot expect in the foreseeable future to be close to the Soviet regime. It must continue to regard the Soviet Union as a rival, not a partner, in the political arena. It must continue to expect that Soviet policies will reflect no abstract love of peace and stability, no real faith in the possibility of a permanent happy coexistence of the communist and capitalist worlds. Rather, Soviet policies will be a cautious, persistent pressure toward the disruption and weakening of all rival influence and rival power.

Source D: The front cover of the propaganda comic book *Is This Tomorrow*, published in America in 1947

IS THIS TOMORROW

AMERICA UNDER COMMUNISM!

Source E: The Truman Doctrine, 12 March 1947

I believe that it must be the policy of the United States to support people who resist being enslaved by armed minorities or by outside pressure. I believe that we must help free peoples to work out their own destiny in their own way.

Source F: A US cartoon of 1949 commenting on the Marshall Plan

I LOVE THE GUY, BUT SOMETIMES I THINK HE'S TOO GOOD!

U.S. TAXPAYER

TO ALL PARTS OF THE WORLD

The Truman Doctrine

From 1946 Truman's government gave up any attempt to continue the wartime co-operation with the Soviet Union. Believing that Stalin intended to build an empire that extended from Eastern to Western Europe, Truman's government decided to contain communism to prevent its expansion beyond the iron curtain. When, in 1947, the US government decided to financially support the government of Greece in its fight against communism, Truman publicly announced the US policy of containment (see Source E).

Moreover, Truman was convinced that communism thrived in places where people faced poverty and hardship. He accepted the advice of General Marshall, who suggested that the USA should help European countries to rebuild their economies, and more than $14 billion was given. This was known as the **Marshall Plan** and it worsened the Cold War rivalry because Stalin refused to allow countries in Eastern Europe to accept this aid.

Tasks

3. *What can you learn from Source C about US attitudes to the Soviet Union in 1946? (For guidance on answering this type of question, see page 16.)*

4. *Study Sources B and D. How reliable are Sources B and D as evidence of Soviet expansion after 1945? (For guidance on answering this type of question, see pages 89–90.)*

The events of 1948–49

The US fear of communism intensified due to the Berlin Crisis of 1948–49. After the Second World War Germany had been divided into four different zones, each controlled by one of the Allies (France, Britain, the USA and the Soviet Union). Berlin sat within the Soviet zone but had also been divided into four sectors, again under the control of the four Allies. In 1948–49, Stalin seemed prepared to risk war in the hope of removing the Allies from Berlin by blockading all road, rail and canal routes into the German capital. The Allies responded with the Berlin airlift of supplies, which eventually forced Stalin to call off the blockade.

These events, and the Soviet development of the atom bomb, convinced the Americans that Stalin wanted world domination. In 1949 the Western countries formed the North Atlantic Treaty Organisation (NATO), which stated that an attack on any NATO member was seen as an attack on the whole alliance. The 'Cold War' was now being waged between the two **Superpowers**.

> **Source G:** A US cartoon of 1948, during the Berlin crisis, showing Berlin being encircled by the Russian bear

The Korean War

Until 1949, US fears of communism had been confined to Europe. However, the success of the Communist Party in China in 1949 indicated the 'danger' of communism as a truly worldwide threat. As far as Truman and his advisers were concerned, the spread of communism had to be halted. American spies reported to Truman that Stalin was using Cominform to help communists win power in Malaya, Indonesia, the Philippines and Korea.

The invasion of South Korea by communist North Korea – supported by China and the Soviet Union – in 1950 seemed to confirm all these fears. There was a wave of anti-communist hysteria in the USA. The **United Nations** sent an international force of overwhelmingly American forces, under the US General MacArthur, to support South Korea. World events had woken up many Americans to the threat of communism, and some of these people now saw a threat within the USA.

> **Source H: From Truman's memoirs, written in 1956**
>
> *This was not the first time the strong had attacked the weak. I remembered Manchuria, Ethiopia, Austria. Communism was acting in Korea just as Hitler, Mussolini and the Japanese had acted earlier. I felt certain that if South Korea was allowed to fall, communist leaders would be encouraged to conquer countries nearer to our shores. No smaller nations would have the courage to resist threats and aggression by stronger communist neighbours.*

Tasks

5. *What can you learn from Source E (on page 9) about the US policy of containment? (For guidance on answering this type of question, see page 16.)*

6. *Study Source F (on page 9) and use your own knowledge. Why was this cartoon published? Use details from the cartoon and your own knowledge to explain the answer. (For guidance on answering this type of question, see page 23.)*

7. *Study Sources G and H. How useful are Sources G and H as evidence of US fears of communist expansion? (For guidance on answering this type of question, see pages 72–73.)*

8. *Which of the following events do you think did most to increase the fear of communism in the USA in the years 1945–50? Place them in rank order from the most to the least.*
- *Soviet expansion in Eastern Europe*
- *the Berlin Blockade*
- *the Soviet testing of the atomic bomb*
- *the communist takeover in China*
- *the Korean War.*

2

The development of the Red Scare

Source A: From Mike Hammer, a fictional private detective in the novel *One Lonely Night*, written by Mickey Spillane in 1951. The novel was a best-seller.

I killed more people tonight than I have fingers on my hands. I shot them in cold blood and enjoyed every minute of it. They were Commies. They were red son-of-bitches who should have died long ago. They never thought that there were people like me in this country. They figured us all to be soft as horse manure and just as stupid.

Task

What can you learn from Source A about US attitudes to communism in 1951?
(For guidance on answering this type of question, see page 16.)

Hatred of communism was further fuelled by events in the USA itself, most notably the cases of the Hollywood Ten, Alger Hiss and the Rosenbergs. Organisations such as the Federal Bureau of Investigation (**FBI**) and the House Un-American Activities Committee (HUAC) investigated anyone thought to be associated with communism.

This chapter will answer the following questions:

• Why did events in the USA, 1945–50, increase the fear of communism?
• What was the importance of the Hiss and Rosenberg cases?

Examination skills

In this chapter you will be given guidance on how to answer the inference question, which is worth six marks.

Why did events in the USA, 1945–50, increase the fear of communism?

The fear of communism was intensified by developments in the USA in the years after 1945 and was known as the 'Red Scare', a name that dated back to the almost hysterical reaction from many US citizens to the Bolshevik Revolution in Russia in October 1917. The Bolsheviks were communists whose symbol was the red flag.

'The enemy within'

President Truman disliked communism and he often talked about 'the enemy within' – meaning inside the USA. His reaction in March 1947 to some congressmen's accusations that he was soft on communists in the USA was to introduce the Federal Employee Loyalty Programme (FELP). FELP was designed to check the security risks of people working in government. Although the checks did not uncover any cases of spying, by 1952 more than 6.6 million federal workers had been examined. Around 3,000 were forced to resign and more than 200 were sacked.

The FBI

The Federal Bureau of Investigation (FBI) had a strong anti-communist director, J. Edgar Hoover. He was the driving influence behind the FELP, and used it to investigate government employees to see if they were members of the Communist Party.

The Hollywood Ten

Later in 1947, the House Un-American Activities Committee (HUAC) began to look into communist infiltration in the film industry. There was a fear that films were being used to put over a communist message. Ten writers and directors had to testify before HUAC, and they were asked if they had ever been members of the Communist Party. They refused to answer, pleading the **Fifth Amendment**. The result was jail, because they were found to be in contempt of **Congress**. The 'Hollywood Ten' were sacked and spent a year in prison.

Source A: J. Edgar Hoover, speaking in 1947

Communism, in reality, is not a political party. It is a way of life, an evil and malignant way of life. It reveals a condition akin to a disease that spreads like an epidemic and, like an epidemic, a quarantine is necessary to keep it from infecting the nation.

Source B: A photograph, taken in October 1947, showing leading Hollywood actors and actresses protesting against the prosecution of the Hollywood Ten

Tasks

1. *What can you learn from Source A about Hoover's attitude to communism? (For guidance on answering this type of question, see page 16.)*

2. *Study Source B and use your own knowledge. Why do you think the photograph was taken? Use details from the photograph and your own knowledge to explain the answer. (For guidance on answering this type of question, see page 23.)*

What was the importance of the Hiss and Rosenberg cases?

The Red Scare gathered momentum due to the impact of two high-profile court cases involving Alger Hiss and the Rosenbergs.

Alger Hiss

Whittaker Chambers, an editor on *Time* magazine and a former communist, informed a leading member of HUAC, Richard Nixon, that Alger Hiss was a spy. Hiss had worked for a **Supreme Court** judge, was at Yalta with Roosevelt and in 1948 was working for a peace organisation. Hiss was interrogated and discredited by Nixon, but there was little evidence to prove him to be a spy.

Later that year, Nixon and one of his assistants were invited to Chambers' farm. Chambers had previously insisted that there had never been any espionage between himself and Hiss. However, at the farm, Chambers suddenly took Nixon and his aide to a pumpkin patch, pulled off the top of a pumpkin and took out a roll of microfilm. The microfilm had government documents, some of which had been copied on Hiss' typewriter. The documents became known as the 'Pumpkin Papers'. In 1950, Hiss was tried for perjury and sentenced to five years in jail – and Nixon became known as a relentless pursuer of communists.

Source B: **Whittaker Chambers speaking before the HUAC in 1948, accusing Hiss of being a spy**

Source A: **Alger Hiss testifying to the HUAC in 1948**

Task

1. *How useful are Sources A and B as evidence of the Hiss Case? Explain your answer using the sources and your own knowledge. (For guidance on answering this type of question, see pages 72–73.)*

The Rosenbergs

Source C: **A photograph of Julius and Ethel Rosenberg in happier times**

The fear of communism continued to grow because the Soviet Union had exploded its first atom bomb in August 1949, several years sooner than the USA had expected. Some in America believed that only spies could have helped them achieve this so quickly. That same month, Julius Rosenberg was arrested on suspicion of spying, and was later tried on the charge of conspiring to commit espionage. His wife, Ethel, was arrested in August of that year on the same charges. The couple had been members of the Communist Party but had no links by 1949. The government claimed that they were intending to give atomic secrets to the Soviet Union. Both were found guilty and sentenced to death. They spent two years on death row and their appeals failed. They were executed on the same day in June 1953.

Source E: **Judge Irving Kaufman, when sentencing the Rosenbergs to death in April 1951**

Your crime is worse than murder, for you put into the hands of the Russians the A-bomb years before our best scientists predicted Russia would perfect the bomb. This has already caused, in my opinion, the communist aggression in Korea, with the resultant casualties exceeding 50,000. Who knows but what that millions more innocent people may pay the price of your treason? Indeed, by your betrayal, you undoubtedly have altered the course of history to the disadvantage of our country.

Source D: **A diagram used by the prosecution in the Rosenberg case, showing the spy ring that reputedly involved the Rosenbergs**

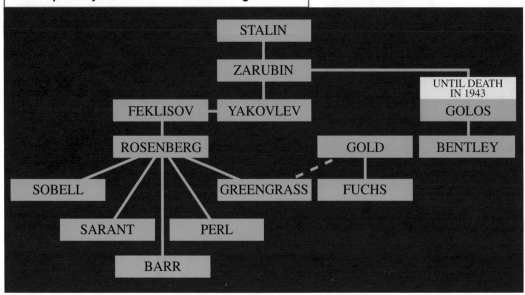

In September 1950, at the height of the Hiss case, and just after the Rosenberg case and the worry over Korea, Congress passed the McCarran Internal Security Act. This meant:

- The Communist Party had to register with the justice department to ensure that the party and its members could be carefully monitored.
- In the event of war, suspected communists could be held in detention camps.
- A Subversive Activities Control Board was set up to watch communist activities in the USA.
- Communists were not allowed to work in armament factories.

Source F: A group of Americans protesting against the Rosenbergs in 1953

Tasks

2. *How useful are Sources D and E as evidence of the Rosenberg Case? Explain your answer using the sources and your own knowledge.* **(For guidance on answering this type of question, see pages 72–73.)**

3. *Study Source F and use your own knowledge. Why were photographs like this published so widely in the USA? Use details from the photograph and your own knowledge to explain the answer.* **(For guidance on answering this type of question, see page 23.)**

4. *Conduct further research of your own and then put forward a case that both Hiss and the Rosenbergs were framed.*

5. *Using Chapters 1 and 2, construct a timeline from 1945–54, as shown below, which shows the key events in the fear of communism in the USA. Place events outside the USA on the top line and internal events ('the enemy within') below the line. Some events have been given as examples.*

US drop atom
bomb on Japan

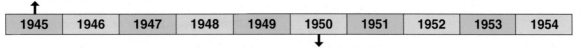

| 1945 | 1946 | 1947 | 1948 | 1949 | 1950 | 1951 | 1952 | 1953 | 1954 |

McCarran Act

Examination practice

This section provides guidance on how to answer the inference question from Unit 3, which is worth six marks.

Question 1 – inference

What can you learn from Source A about the Rosenbergs?

> **Source A: From a statement made by President Eisenhower on 19 June 1953, the day of the execution of the Rosenbergs**
>
> *I am not unmindful of the fact that this case has aroused grave concern both here and abroad. In this connection I can only say that, by immeasurably increasing the chances of atomic war, the Rosenbergs may have condemned to death tens of millions of innocent people all over the world. The execution of two human beings is a grave matter. But even graver is the thought of millions of dead, whose death may be directly attributable to what these spies have done.*

The source suggests that the Rosenbergs had received much support in the USA and throughout the world. Eisenhower stresses the concern felt at home and abroad.

> **Source A**
> I am not unmindful of the fact that this case has aroused grave concern both here and abroad. In this connection I can only say that, by immeasurably increasing the chances of atomic war, the Rosenbergs may have condemned to death tens of millions of innocent people all over the world. The execution of two human beings is a grave matter…

Eisenhower suggests that the Rosenbergs have increased the likelihood of a nuclear conflict when he mentions the possibility of atomic war.

The president seems to be trying to justify the execution by suggesting their actions will lead to the death of millions.

How to answer

- You are being asked to give messages from the source, to read between the lines of what is written.
- In addition, you must support the inference. In other words, use details from the source to support the messages you say it gives.
- Begin your answer with 'Source … suggests that …' In this way you will make a judgement and avoid repeating the contents of the source.
- Look for key words in the source that might lead to inferences. You could tackle this by highlighting different messages in the source (as in the example opposite).
- You need at least two supported inferences (see the examples for Source A opposite).

Now have a go yourself

Try answering question 2 using the steps shown for question 1.

Question 2 – inference

What can you learn from Source B about the Hiss case?

> **Source B: From a telegram sent by Alger Hiss to the House Un-American Activities Committee (HUAC) in 1948. He was responding to the accusations made by Whittaker Chambers.**
>
> *I do not know Mr Chambers and, so far as I am aware, have never laid eyes on him. There is no basis for the statements made by Mr Whittaker about me to your House of Un-American Activities Committee. I would further appreciate the opportunity of appearing before your committee to answer these statements.*

3

The Impact of McCarthyism

Source A: A cartoon in the *Washington Post*, 1954. The figure represents Joe McCarthy.

Source B: From a speech by Senator Joe McCarthy, January 1950

While I cannot take the time to name all the men in the State Department who have been named as members of the Communist Party and members of a spy ring, I have here in my hand a list of 205 that are known to the Secretary of State as being members of the Communist Party and are still working and shaping the policy of the State Department.

Tasks

1. *What is the message of the cartoon?*

2. *What can you learn from Source B about McCarthy's methods? (Remember how to answer this type of question? For further guidance, see page 16.)*

In 1950, an ambitious and dishonest **Republican senator**, Joe McCarthy, claimed he had a list of 205 members of the Communist Party of the United States who worked for the State Department (see Source B). This man, who was the nation's most ardent anti-communist, became the symbol of the 'Red-hating crusader' and gave his name to the era – McCarthyism. Over the next few years McCarthyism became associated with a communist witch hunt, in which over 2,000 men and women were summoned to appear before the Senate's House Un-American Activities Committee. By the time he was exposed as a fraud and liar, he had created an atmosphere of fear and ruined the lives of many.

This chapter will answer the following questions:

• Why was McCarthy able to win support?
• Why did McCarthyism fade away?
• What were the effects of McCarthyism?

Examination skills

In this chapter you will be given guidance on how to answer the source interpretation question which is worth eight marks.

Why was McCarthy able to win support?

McCarthy showing the amount of communist activity in the USA in 1954.

Source A: From President Truman's speech rejecting the McCarran Bill, 1950

There is no more basic truth in American life than the statement – 'In a free country we punish men for the crimes they commit but not for the opinions they have.'

At the height of the fears in 1950, there appeared a senator who in a very short time created hysteria about communism. This was Senator Joseph McCarthy of Wisconsin.

On 9 February 1950, McCarthy addressed a Republican meeting in West Virginia and stated that he had the names of 205 communists who were working in the State Department, which dealt with foreign affairs. He also cited Owen Lattimore, a professor at one of the top US universities, as the 'top Russian spy'. Over the following weeks his claims fluctuated, leading some people to question whether they could be supported. No names were produced apart from Lattimore's, and even he was cleared of any wrong-doing in 1955.

A **Senate** committee was set up to investigate the accusations, and after several weeks it decided that McCarthy's claims were 'a fraud and a hoax'. The committee chairman, Senator Tydings, was branded a communist by McCarthy and in the autumn he was defeated in the Senate elections by a supporter of McCarthy. From this point, many politicians were frightened to speak out against him.

It was in this atmosphere that the McCarran Act (see page 15) was passed, despite President Truman's attempts to veto it (see Source A).

Some Congressmen jumped on the McCarthy bandwagon, and the HUAC continued to seek out those who would undermine the USA. The attack on Hollywood continued (see page 12), and many actors and writers were blacklisted and were unable to secure work for several years – in some cases ever again. It is estimated that there were about 50 films made between 1947 and 1954 that openly showed communists as enemies of the USA.

The media did much to intensify the fear of communism. The Cold War hit the movies in 1948 with the film *The Iron Curtain*, which told the story of a clerk in the Russian embassy in Ottawa who defected to the West. Over the next decade a succession of films – some bordering on hysteria, such as *I Married a Communist* (1950) – seemed to show communist subversion everywhere in US society.

Source B: The advertisement for the 1948 film *The Iron Curtain*

McCarthy's influence

McCarthy was made Chairman of the Government Committee on Operations of the Senate, a position that allowed him to investigate state bodies and also interview hundreds of individuals about their political beliefs. His aim was to root out communists from the government, and his hearings and public statements destroyed the lives of many people. Little evidence was produced – it was enough to simply be accused by him. Nevertheless, he won massive support across the USA and it is clear that in late 1952, his activities contributed to the Republicans' presidential victory.

Nixon, as vice-presidential candidate, was quick to build on the hysteria created by McCarthy (see Source C). For Nixon, the issue would be a vote-winner not only for the Republicans but also for himself.

McCarthy continued his work of hunting out communists and, in late 1952, his researchers investigated libraries to see whether they contained any anti-American books that might have been written by communists. As a result of the searches, many of these books were taken out of circulation.

Source E: Philip Reed, Head of General Electric, writing to President Eisenhower on 8 June 1953, describing how some European countries were concerned about the impact of McCarthyism inside the USA. Reed was head of one of the most powerful companies in the USA, and after a visit to Europe he was concerned that the USA might find itself losing European customers. The memory of the Second World War was still very strong, and at the height of the Cold War, the USA could not afford to lose allies.

I urge you to take issue with McCarthy and make it stick. People in high and low places see in him a potential Hitler … That he could get away with what he already has in America has made some of them wonder whether our concept of democratic government and the rights of individuals is really different from those of the communist and fascists.

Source C: From a speech by Richard Nixon, Republican vice-president candidate, September 1952, indicating his intentions about the communist threat

What I intend to do is go up and down this land … and expose the communists and crooks and those that defend them until they are all thrown out of Washington.

Source D: Harry S. Truman, speaking on the radio, 17 November 1953, about his views on McCarthyism

McCarthyism … the meaning of the word is the corruption of the truth, the abandonment of our historical devotion to fair play. It is the abandonment of 'due process' of law. It is the use of the big lie and the unfounded accusation against any citizen in the name of Americanism and security ... This horrible cancer is eating at the vitals of America and it can destroy the great edifice of freedom.

Tasks

1. *How far do Sources A, C and D agree about McCarthyism? (For guidance on answering this type of question, see pages 60–61.)*

2. *How useful is Source B as evidence of the development of the Red Scare in the USA? (For guidance on answering this type of question, see pages 72–73.)*

3. *What can you learn from Source E about McCarthyism? (Remember how to answer this type of question? For further guidance, see page 16.)*

4. *Why was McCarthy able to win the support of many US people so quickly?*

5. *Working in pairs, put forward a list of reasons why McCarthyism seemed to contradict the basic ideas of a free and open society.*

Why did McCarthyism fade away?

The role of President Eisenhower

Even though McCarthy was a Republican, this did not prevent him from attacking his own party after the presidential election. The new president, Eisenhower, had done little to challenge him, and McCarthy seemed to think he could attack anyone with impunity. He objected to President Eisenhower's choice of ambassador to the Soviet Union (Charles Bohlen), but was overruled by a special Senate committee.

Eisenhower and his government dealt with the communist threat in their own way. A Federal Loyalty Programme, similar to that of Truman's administration (see page 12), was introduced and then the Communist Control Act was passed. This limited the legal rights of the party and made membership extremely difficult.

The role of the army

McCarthy sealed his own fate when he began to cast doubts about the security of the army. His investigations were televised from April to June 1954 and, in these, the American public saw for the first time the true nature of the man. He never produced any hard evidence, relying instead on bluster and bluff. Furthermore, McCarthy was very aggressive in his questioning of witnesses – some felt he bullied in his cross-examinations. The army attorney, Joseph Welch, approached the hearing in a calm and measured manner, in contrast to McCarthy. The claims against the army were seen to be unfounded and McCarthy himself now faced challenges.

The role of the media

There had already been a television programme in March 1954 that condemned McCarthy. The acclaimed journalist Ed Murrow (see Source A), produced a programme based almost entirely on McCarthy's words, and this showed clearly the shabby nature of all the baseless claims.

> **Source A: Ed Murrow, a leading American journalist, 9 March 1954, attacking McCarthyism**
>
> *The line between investigating and persecuting is a very fine one and … [McCarthy] has stepped over it repeatedly. This is no time for those who oppose him to keep quiet.*

Other journalists began to attack McCarthy (see Source B) and, at last, those who had feared him now found the confidence to express their views openly.

> **Source B: *Louisville Courier-Journal*, 1954, attacking McCarthyism**
>
> *In this long, degrading distortion of the democratic process McCarthy has shown himself to be evil and unmatched in malice.*

McCarthy's fall

In December 1954, McCarthy was publicly reprimanded by the Senate for:

- contempt of a Senate elections sub-committee
- abuse of certain senators
- insults to the Senate during the very hearings that condemned him.

The vote was 67–22 in favour of censuring him. (Only one **Democrat** did not vote for reprimand – John F. Kennedy.)

McCarthy then lost the chairmanship of the Committee on Operations of the Senate, and this signalled the end of his power. For many, his death in 1957 was not a time for mourning.

Source C: A cartoon about McCarthy, 1954

ACCUSATIONS

Source D: From an article in the *Chicago Tribune*, May 1957

Senator McCarthy was a patriotic American and a determined opponent of Communists. And because of that every 'liberal' commentator lost no opportunity to vilify him. No man in public life was ever persecuted and maligned because of his beliefs as was Senator McCarthy.

Source E: From *The Glory and the Dream*, written in 1974 by William Manchester, a US historian

He was a rogue, and he looked the part. His eyes were shifty. When he laughed, he snickered. His voice as a high-pitch taunt. What he had going for him was a phenomenal ability to lie and an intuitive grasp of the American communications system. That and ruthlessness. He enjoyed reading his name in newspapers and he wanted to remain a senator.

Tasks

1. *Study Source C and use your own knowledge. What is the purpose of the cartoon? Use details from the cartoon and your own knowledge to explain the answer. (For guidance on answering this type of question, see page 23.)*

2. *Draw a post-McCarthy poster warning Americans about the dangers of the spread of communism in the USA.*

3. *How far do sources A, D and E support the view that McCarthyism was justified? (For guidance on answering this type of question, see pages 60–61.)*

4. *Why did McCarthyism cease to have a hold on the American people?*

What were the effects of McCarthyism?

McCarthy's brief time as 'Communist-finder General' had divided the USA, and his influence lived on after him.

- The words 'red', 'pinko', 'commie' and 'lefty' became synonymous with someone who was politically unsound, unpatriotic and therefore a threat to the USA.
- McCarthy had created a climate of fear, and with the Cold War still raging in the 1950s it was difficult for people to overcome their fears. There was much spying on neighbours, and government films encouraged people to expose anyone who was thought to have communist sympathies.

- Anyone who sought to change the USA, for example by bringing in **civil rights** for black Americans, was seen as a communist.
- The hatred of communism never died away.

Abroad, the communist threat did seem to have diminished a little and the world situation seemed to be changing gradually after 1953. Stalin had died and his replacement, Nikita Khrushchev, was prepared to improve East–West relations. An **armistice** had helped to bring hostilities in the Korean War to a close – communism seemed to have been contained.

Nevertheless, the climate of fear still existed within the USA and can best be seen in Arthur Miller's play *The Crucible* (1953). Although it was written at the height of the communist hysteria, the play has never lost popularity. Furthermore, the 1955 film *Invasion of the Body Snatchers* proved to be successful in warning Americans of the dangers of people such as Joe McCarthy.

Source A: **A poster for the 1955 film *Invasion of the Body Snatchers*, which warned of the dangers of McCarthyism. The science-fiction film depicted aliens taking over the bodies of humans so that they could not be recognised.**

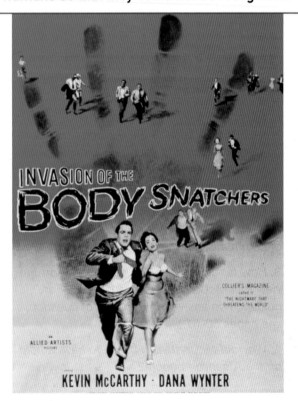

Tasks

1. *Study Source A. Why do you think some people interpreted this film as a warning against communism?*

2. *How useful is Source A as evidence of the fear of communism in the USA in the mid-1950s? (For guidance on answering this type of question, see pages 72–73.)*

3. *'Reds Under the Bed'. This was a famous anti-communist headline of the 1950s in the USA. Working with a partner, put together three or four anti-communist headlines.*

4. *What were the effects of McCarthyism on the people of the USA?*

Examination practice

This section provides guidance on how to answer the source interpretation question from Unit 3, which is worth eight marks.

Question 1 – source interpretation

Study Source A and use your own knowledge. What was the purpose of this cartoon? Use details from the cartoon and your own knowledge to explain your answer.

How to answer

You are being asked to explain why the source was produced. In order to do this you need to:

- Examine carefully the details of the source and use these to back up your answer.
- Make inferences from the source. What is it suggesting? What is its tone or attitude? What is the overall message? Use details from the source to back up your answer.

- Why does it have this message? What is it trying to make you think? Is it trying to get you to support or oppose a person or event? Use details from the source to back up your answer.
- Support your answer on the purpose of the source with your own contextual knowledge. In other words, your knowledge of what was going on at that time that involves the person or event. In this case you can explain about some or all of the following:
- attitudes to communists at this time
- impact of Hiss and Rosenberg cases
- Korean War and fears of communism.

To plan an answer to this question, you could annotate the source as shown below. Part of an answer showing how to support the inferences from the source with contextual knowledge is also given below.

Overall message
There are many US citizens who are communists.

Purpose
To increase the fear of communism in the USA and possibly win support for McCarthy and his methods.

Inference
Communists are evil.

Inference
Many communists are working for the US government.

Details
An American swearing an oath of loyalty. He looks evil. Hammer and Sickle on back, which is symbol of Soviet flag.

Source A: An American cartoon of the early 1950s

Source A suggests that communists are evil, as the person swearing the communist oath is made to look like a monster. Moreover, these people are working for the American government and swearing an oath of loyalty. Overall, the message of the source is that communism is widespread in the USA. This source was produced during the Red Scare when the Cold War in Europe and Asia, and the Hiss and Rosenberg cases in America, were encouraging a fear of communism in the USA.
The purpose of the source is to increase the fear of communism in the USA and possibly win support for McCarthy and his methods.

Key Topic 2: The civil rights movement, 1945–62

Source A: A cartoon from the *Washington Post*, August 1960

Task

Study Source A. What message is the cartoonist trying to put across?

This key topic examines the growth of the **civil rights** movement from the end of the Second World War to the presidency of John F. Kennedy. There was some real progress during the 1950s, and decisions made by the **Supreme Court** were crucial to the advances that were made. By the early 1960s the civil rights movement had found a charismatic leader who could not be ignored – Martin Luther King.

Each chapter explains a key issue and examines important lines of enquiry, as outlined below:

Chapter 4 Progress in civil rights (pages 25–34)
- What was the impact of the Second World War on civil rights?
- What was the work of the NAACP and CORE?
- What were the key developments in education in the years to 1962?

Chapter 5 The Montgomery Bus Boycott (pages 35–44)
- What were the causes of the Montgomery Bus Boycott?
- What were the events of the Bus Boycott?
- What was the role of Martin Luther King?
- What was the importance of the Bus Boycott?

Chapter 6 Martin Luther King and progress and problems, 1958–62 (pages 45–53)
- What was the impact of the Civil Rights Act, 1957?
- What part did sit-ins play in civil rights?
- Who were the 'freedom riders'?
- What progress had been made by 1962?

Source A: A segregated cinema in the USA, 1943. Notice the barrier dividing the seats.

Source B: The body of Cleo Wright, a black man who was burned by a mob after being taken from custody of officers, is observed by a crowd in Missouri, 1942. The victim was suspected of the attempted rape of a white woman.

Task

Study Sources A and B. What can you learn from the photographs about attitudes to black Americans during the war?

Racial **discrimination** was a common feature of everyday life in the USA before the Second World War. Black Americans experienced **segregation** and discrimination in all walks of life. When war broke out, there was increased optimism that things would change. After all, if the USA was fighting fascism and racism, how could it continue to discriminate and deny civil rights to large sections of its own population? By the early 1960s some positive changes had occurred, mainly in education and transport – but there was still much to do.

This chapter answers the following questions:

- What was the impact of the Second World War on civil rights?
- What was the work of the NAACP and CORE?
- What were the key developments in education in the years to 1962?

Examination skills

In this chapter you will be given further guidance on how to answer the source interpretation question, which is worth eight marks.

What was the impact of the Second World War on civil rights?

The Second World War did provide some opportunities for black Americans and, as a result, a few aspects of life improved. The mobilisation of US industry created employment, and hundreds of thousands of black Americans moved from the South to the North. There were higher wages and many became skilled workers. Moreover, there was the chance to serve in the armed forces – but those who did serve found continued discrimination.

Source A: Black American soldiers in action in 1944, during the Second World War

Black Americans and the armed forces

There were few advances in civil rights during the Second World War (1941–45). Segregation existed in the armed forces, where black Americans performed the menial tasks and found promotion difficult. When black soldiers were injured, only blood from black soldiers could be used because many whites felt that to mix blood would 'mongrelise' the USA. The war highlighted the racism and discrimination in the armed forces, which was ironic because the USA was fighting against a racist state, Nazi Germany. Black soldiers stationed in Britain were treated far better than those back home. In the army, there were black-only units with white officers. Before 1944, black soldiers were not allowed into combat in the

Source B: This 'prayer' appeared in a black newspaper in January 1943

Draftee's Prayer
*Dear Lord, today
I go to war:
To fight, to die
Tell me what for
Dear Lord, I'll fight,
I do not fear
Germans or Japs,
My fears are here.
America.*

marines. They were employed to transport supplies, or as cooks and labourers. Many black women served in the armed forces as nurses but were only allowed to treat black soldiers. The US air force would not accept black pilots.

Discrimination was worst in the navy, with black soldiers given the most dangerous job of loading ammunition on ships bound for war zones. For example, in 1944 a horrific accident killed 323 people – most of them black sailors. Few became officers.

Tasks

1. *Study Source A and use your own knowledge. Why do you think this photograph was published in the USA in 1944? Use details from the photograph and your own knowledge to explain the answer. (Remember how to answer this type of question? For further guidance, see page 23.)*

2. *What can you learn from Source B about the fears of the black American soldier? (Remember how to answer this type of question? For further guidance, see page 16.)*

3. *In what ways had black American soldiers made gains during the Second World War?*

The reaction to this among black soldiers was to push for a 'Double V' campaign – victory for civil rights at home as well as militarily abroad. Gradually there was change, supported by the US Supreme Commander, General Eisenhower:

- In the air force, by the end of 1945, 600 black pilots had been trained, although they were not allowed to fly in the same groups as whites.
- There were some mixed units in the army during the **Battle of the Bulge** (late 1944).
- By the end of 1944, there were almost three quarters of a million black Americans in the US army.
- In early 1945, the navy had more than 165,000 ratings who were no longer limited to menial positions.
- **Desegregation** in the navy came in 1946, and following Executive Order 9981 in 1948, segregation in the other forces came to an end.

By the end of the war, 58 black sailors had risen to the rank of officer.

Black Americans and employment

In 1941, Philip Randolph, a leading black American fighting for equality, sought to remove discrimination in the armed forces and the workplace. He organised the March on Washington Movement, and used the slogan 'We loyal Americans demand the right to work and fight for our country'. This was to be a mass march on Washington together with a possible strike to try and make the government bring an end to discrimination in the workplace. The government was alarmed at the possibility of a mass strike and came up with a compromise:

- Randolph called off the march.
- Roosevelt issued Executive Order 8802, which not only stopped discrimination in industrial and government jobs, but also set up the Fair Employment Practices Commission (FEPC) to prevent discrimination at work.

As a result, the numbers of black Americans employed in government service increased from 50,000 to 200,000, and by the end of the war there were more than two million black Americans involved in industry.

> **Source C: From *Mr Black Labour*, by the historian D. Davis, 1972, quoting the president of the North American Aviation Company in 1942**
>
> *While we are in complete sympathy with the Negro, it is against company policy to employ them as aircraft workers or mechanics, regardless of their training, but there will be some jobs as janitors for Negroes.*

The war also meant a broadening of opportunities for black American women. The number who worked in domestic service fell from 75 per cent to less than 50 per cent by 1945. Many became nurses, but they were only permitted to help black American soldiers.

Source D: Black female Americans working in the arms industry during the war.

Source E: A skilled black American worker involved in the construction of an aircraft carrier

Source F: A notice in Detroit during the riots of 1943

Over 400,000 black Americans migrated from the South to the USA's industrial centres, where they continued to face discrimination and prejudice. Black workers generally only earned half of what white workers earned. This led to racial tension, and there were race riots in 47 cities, the worst of which was in Detroit in 1943. During this riot, the city was put under martial law. On 21 June, 25 black and nine white people were killed. More than 700 people were injured and there was $2 million worth of damage to property.

In the same year, nine black Americans were killed in riots in Harlem, New York.

By the end of the war, there was an increased awareness in the US Government of the problems faced by black Americans – but there was no attempt to address any of the issues. Many black American soldiers returning from the war felt let down when they still faced discrimination and a society that treated them as inferior. After 1945, moves to improve civil rights were slow, piecemeal and not always successful.

Tasks

4. *How far do Sources C, D (page 27) and E agree about the employment of black Americans during the Second World War? (For guidance on answering this type of question, see pages 60–61.)*

5. *In what ways did the Second World War help black Americans improve employment opportunities?*

6. *What can you learn from Source F about race relations in the USA during the Second World War? (Remember how to answer this type of question? For further guidance, see page 16.)*

What was the work of the NAACP and CORE?

The National Association for the Advancement of Colored People (NAACP)

The NAACP had been founded in 1909 by a group of leading black intellectuals. The organisation was multi-racial and had W.E.B. du Bois as a leading member. Du Bois was one of the most important figures in the campaign for civil rights in the first half of the twentieth century. He was an intellectual and an activist. The main aim of the NAACP was 'to ensure the political, educational, social and economic equality of rights of all persons and to eliminate racial hatred and racial discrimination'. The NAACP sought to use all legal means to achieve equality.

Growing awareness of discrimination and its injustice led to a growth in membership of the NAACP – from 50,000 in 1940 to 450,000 by 1945. Many of the new members were professionals, but there were also many new urban workers. This organisation played an important part in the civil rights movement, because it raised the profile of issues not only within the black community but also the white one. Moreover, it encouraged many black Americans to become active in the quest for civil rights.

Congress of Racial Equality (CORE)

In 1942, a new organisation was founded by James Farmer, a young black American activist. He called it the **Congress of Racial Equality**. CORE was inspired by the non-violent tactics of Gandhi in India. It employed the idea of **sit-ins** at cinemas and restaurants to highlight the issue of segregation, and it led to the end of this practice in some northern cities. It also began to demand the end of segregation on transport.

The issue of civil rights split the **Democrats** in the 1948 presidential election. Truman was acutely aware of the racial tensions within the USA (see Source A), but he knew that he would have to tread carefully because many of the **Dixiecrats** (Southern Democratic Party politicians) would vote against any of his reforming measures. He wanted to introduce a civil rights bill, and also put forward an anti-**lynching** bill, but both were rejected by the southern Dixiecrats.

> **Source A: From a speech given by President Truman, 18 August 1948, describing his revulsion at lynching**
>
> *I am asking for equality of opportunity for all human beings and as long as I stay here, I shall continue that fight. When the mob gangs can take four people and shoot them in the back and everybody in the country is acquainted with who did the shooting and nothing is done about it, that country is in a pretty bad fix.*

By the end of the decade, those seeking improved civil rights had made only modest gains. There had been some progress in employment and the armed forces, and many blacks had become more active in campaigning for civil rights. On the other hand, discrimination and segregation remained a way of life in the southern states, whilst the migration of many black Americans to the industrial cities of the North had created greater racial tension.

Another pressure group, the **Student Non-violent Co-ordinating Committee** (SNCC), was formed in 1960 and comprised more radical young people (see page 48).

Tasks

1. *How useful is Source A as evidence of the problems black Americans faced? Explain your answer.*

2. *Re-read pages 26–28. Was there any progress in civil rights for black Americans in the 1940s? Construct a balance sheet, showing progress on one side and a lack of progress on the other.*

A photograph of segregated water fountains in the American South during the 1950s.

In the 1950s, segregation was still a key feature of life for black Americans, and they were subject to what were known as the 'Jim Crow' laws. These were laws passed in the southern states at the end of the nineteenth century to segregate blacks from whites in daily life. The Supreme Court had ruled in the Plessy v. Ferguson case of 1896 that if separate conditions for blacks and whites were equal, then segregation was constitutional. This became the 'separate but equal' doctrine – and it was to be challenged in the 1950s.

Brown v. Topeka Board of Education, 1954

The first case to challenge segregation did not originate in the South, but in the Midwest state of Kansas. Linda Brown's parents wanted her to attend a neighbourhood school rather than the school for black Americans, which was some distance away. Lawyers from the NACCP (led by Thurgood Marshall) presented evidence to the Supreme Court, stating that separate education created low self-esteem and was psychologically harmful. Moreover, the evidence also pointed out that educational achievement was restricted because of this policy. The process took eighteen months and the decision was announced on 17 May 1954. Chief Justice Warren of the Supreme Court gave a closing judgement (see Source A).

> **Source A: From the closing judgement of Chief Justice Warren of the Supreme Court at the end of the Brown v. Topeka Case**
>
> *Separating white and coloured children in schools had a detrimental effect upon coloured children. The impact is greater when it has the sanction of the law; for the separating of the races is usually interpreted as denoting the inferiority of the Negro group … We conclude that in the field of public education the doctrine of 'separate but equal' has no place. Separate educational facilities are inherently unequal.*

Problems after Brown v. Topeka

However, the judgement did not specify how integration should be carried out – apart from a vague notion of 'at the earliest possible speed'. Some areas began to desegregate and by 1957, more than 300,000 black children were attending schools that had formerly been segregated.

However, there were 2.4 million black southern children who were still being educated in Jim Crow schools (separate schools for black Americans). Moreover, there were many states, especially in the South, that took deliberate measures to keep separate schools. The **Ku Klux Klan** began to re-emerge and some parents joined **White Citizens' Councils**, which aimed to maintain segregation. More than 100 southern **senators** and congressmen signed the Southern Manifesto, a document that opposed racial integration in education. Over the next two years, southern state legislatures passed more than 450 laws and resolutions aimed at preventing the Brown decision being enforced.

In 1956, the University of Alabama accepted a black student, Autherine Lucy, under a government court order that had been secured by the NAACP. Many white students rioted and the university authorities removed her. She was forbidden to re-enter the university. It was 1963 before black Americans were finally allowed to study there.

Despite the decision of the Supreme Court and the open hostility to the Brown case, President Eisenhower did little to encourage integration. He was forced into action in 1957.

This photograph shows three NAACP lawyers, (from left) George E. C. Hayes, Thurgood Marshall and James Nabrit Jr, celebrating after the Brown verdict.

Tasks

1. *What is meant by the term 'Jim Crow' laws?*

2. *What reasons did Chief Justice Warren give in his dismissal of the Jim Crow laws in Source A?*

3. *Did the Brown case bring progress for the civil rights movement? Copy the table below and complete the boxes, explaining your answers.*

Yes, because…	No, because…

Little Rock High School, 1957

After the Brown decision, Little Rock High School, Arkansas, decided to allow nine black students to enrol there. On 3 September 1957, the nine – led by Elizabeth Eckford – tried to enrol but were prevented by the governor, Orval Faubus, who ordered state National Guardsmen to block their entry. Faubus said there would be public disorder if black students tried to enrol. The following day, 4 September, the National Guard was removed by order of Faubus, and the nine students ran the gauntlet of a vicious white crowd. At midday, the students went home under police guard because their safety could not be guaranteed. Press and television coverage in the USA and across the world was a serious embarrassment to a country that put itself forward as the champion of freedom and equality.

President Eisenhower had to act. He used the National Guard and federal troops to protect the black students for the rest of the school year. Despite the president's intervention, Faubus closed all Arkansas schools the following year, simply to prevent integration.

Many white and most black students had no schooling for a year. Schools in Arkansas re-opened in 1959 following a Supreme Court ruling.

Source C: **Demonstrators against integration in schools in Arkansas, 1959**

Source B: **Black American students arriving at Little Rock High School in a US army car, 1957**

Why was Little Rock significant?

- It involved the president, thus demonstrating that civil rights was an issue that could no longer be ignored.
- It demonstrated that states would be overruled by the **federal government** when necessary.
- The demonstrations were seen on television and in newspapers across the world. It did the USA no good to be seen as an oppressive nation when it was criticising communist countries for not allowing their citizens basic human rights.
- Many US citizens saw, for the first time, the racial hatred that existed in the southern states.
- It did help to moderate some of the views held by white Americans at the time.
- Black activists were beginning to realise that reliance on the federal courts was not enough to secure change.

The James Meredith case

In June 1962, the Supreme Court upheld a federal court decision to force Mississippi University to accept James Meredith. The university did not want any black students and Meredith was prevented from registering. In his first major involvement in civil rights, President Kennedy sent in 320 federal marshals to escort Meredith to the campus. There were riots and two people were killed, 166 marshals and 210 demonstrators were wounded. President Kennedy was forced to send more than 2,000 troops to restore order. The black activists called the event 'The Battle of Oxford'. Three hundred soldiers had to remain on the campus until Meredith received his degree three years later.

There were some other instances of resistance to integration in education, such as that led by Governor Wallace in Alabama, when he tried to stop black Americans from enrolling at the state university. Wallace said, 'I am the embodiment of the sovereignty of this state, and I will be present to bar the entrance of any Negro who attempts to enrol at the university.' However, the fact that there had been federal intervention at Mississippi University showed the tide had turned.

Source D: James Meredith being escorted into Mississippi University by federal marshals and armed soldiers, 1963

Tasks

4. *Why do you think that education played such an important part in the struggle for civil rights in the 1950s?*

5. *Did events at Little Rock High School bring progress for the civil rights movement? Copy the table below and complete the boxes, explaining your answers.*

Yes, because...	No, because...

6. *Write a poem/protest song about events at Little Rock High School.*

7. *How useful are Sources B and D in helping you understand the issues of civil rights in the USA? (For guidance on answering this type of question, see pages 72–73.)*

8. *What can you learn from Source C about attitudes to integration in the USA in 1959? (Remember how to answer this type of question? For further guidance, see page 16.)*

9. *Why was the Meredith case important for the civil rights movement?*

Examination practice

This section provides guidance on how to answer the source interpretation question from Unit 3, which is worth eight marks.

Question – source interpretation

Study Source A and use your own knowledge. What was the purpose of this song? Use details from the song and your own knowledge to explain your answer.

How to answer

You are being asked to explain why the source was produced. In order to do this you need to:

- Examine carefully the details of the source and use these to back up your answer.
- Make inferences from the source. What is it suggesting? What is its tone or attitude? What is the overall message? Use details from the source to back up your answer.

- Why does it have this message? What is it trying to make you think? Is it trying to get you to support or oppose a person or event? Use details from the source to back up your answer.
- Support your answer on the purpose of the source with your own contextual knowledge. In other words, your knowledge of what was going on at that time which involves the person or event. In this case you can explain about some or all of the following:
- racial discrimination
- role of the authorities in allowing violence
- role of the protest singer at this time (see page 87).

To plan an answer to this question, you could annotate the source as shown in the example below.

Now try answering the question using the annotations around the source to help you. See page 23 for an example of how this has been done for another question.

Purpose
To encourage people to see what was happening in education and highlight the injustices of the day.

Inference
Black Americans experienced violence.

Inference
People were killed but no one had looked into it.

Source A: Part of Bob Dylan's song 'Oxford Town'. Dylan was singing about the James Meredith Case. Oxford was the site of Mississippi University.

He went down to Oxford Town
Guns and clubs followed him down
All because his face was brown
Better get away from Oxford Town
Oxford Town around the bend
He come in to the door, he couldn't get in
All because of the colour of his skin
What do you think about that, my frien'?

Oxford Town in the afternoon
Ev'rybody singin' a sorrowful tune
Two men died 'neath the Mississippi moon
Somebody better investigate soon

Oxford Town, Oxford Town
Ev'rybody's got their heads bowed down
The sun don't shine above the ground
Ain't a-goin' down to Oxford Town

Details
This shows that the key issue is racism.

Inference
This shows black Americans could not get into places of education.

Overall message
A dark, depressing place which carries a message of pessimism because of the racism.

34

The Montgomery Bus Boycott

Source A: Verse sung by Montgomery bus boycotters, 1955–56

Ain't gonna ride them buses no more,
Ain't gonna ride no more,
Why don't all the white folk know
That I ain't gonna ride no more.

Task

What do Sources A and B tell you about the Montgomery Bus Boycott?

Source B: A cartoon published in the USA during the Montgomery Bus Boycott

In December 1955, thousands of black residents of Montgomery began a boycott of city buses to protest against racially segregated seating. After 381 days of taking taxis, carpooling and walking, black Americans eventually won their fight to desegregate seating on public transport, not only in Montgomery but across the whole of the USA. The Montgomery Bus Boycott of 1955–56 is often viewed as the defining protest of black Americans. Peaceful protesting, the use of the economic weapon that almost bankrupted the bus company, and the powerful eloquence of Martin Luther King, all secured a definitive victory.

This chapter answers the following questions:

• What were the causes of the Montgomery Bus Boycott?
• What were the events of the Bus Boycott?
• What was the role of Martin Luther King?
• What was the importance of the Bus Boycott?

Examination skills

In this chapter you will be given guidance on how to answer the cross-referencing question, which is worth ten marks.

What were the causes of the Montgomery Bus Boycott?

Segregation on public transport in the USA had long been a problem for black Americans. Attempts to end this had found some success in the early 1950s in Baton Rouge, Louisiana, where, following a ten-day bus boycott, black Americans were allowed to board buses from back to front and whites from front to back. However, blacks were still prohibited from sitting with or in front of white passengers. The transport issue came to a head in Montgomery, Alabama, after the arrest of Rosa Parks in December 1955. The rules about segregation on public transport in Montgomery were particularly harsh:

- Black Americans had to follow the instructions of the white drivers.
- The front part of the bus was reserved for whites at all times.
- Black Americans had to fill the bus from the back.
- Black Americans could not sit next to whites and had to stand even if there was a vacant seat.
- If a white person boarded the bus and all white seats were taken, blacks had to give up their seats.

Background to the boycott

In March 1955 there had been a case where Claudette Colvin, a young black girl, had been arrested for refusing to give up her seat to a white person. The NAACP (see page 29) in Montgomery had considered challenging the segregation laws for some time, but decided to wait for a stronger case (Colvin became pregnant during the time the NAACP was considering her case

and, as she was unmarried, it was felt that this would be seized on by white opponents). The opportunity came in December of that year, when Rosa Parks also refused to surrender her seat. On Thursday 1 December 1955, Parks refused to give up her seat to a white man. She was subsequently arrested and from this point the situation escalated into a crisis.

Parks was the secretary of the local NAACP and knew many influential local activists. Initially, the Montgomery Women's Political Council, led by Jo Ann Robinson, decided to hold a one-day boycott on Monday 5 December, the day of Parks' trial.

Police photograph of Jo Ann Robinson, February 1956, taken at the time of her arrest with Rosa Parks and Martin Luther King.

On the day after Parks' arrest, Robinson and some students printed thousands of leaflets encouraging people to boycott buses.

Source B: **From the speech made by Martin Luther King, 5 December 1955**

We are here this evening to say to those who have mistreated us so long that we are tired – tired of being segregated and humiliated, tired of being kicked about by the brutal feet of oppression. We have sometimes given people the feeling that we liked the way we were being treated. But we come here tonight to be saved from that patience that makes us patient with anything less than freedom and justice ... in our protest there will be no cross burnings ... We will be guided by the highest principles of law and order. Our method will be that of persuasion, not coercion.

Preparation for the boycott

During the weekend, local civil rights activists such as E. D. Nixon, Ralph Abernathy and Martin Luther King Jr. (the new minister at Dexter Avenue Baptist Church) became involved. They began to plan a rally for the evening of the trial and the local NAACP started preparing its legal challenge to the segregation laws. At the meeting, the Montgomery Improvement Association (MIA) was established to oversee the continuation and maintenance of the boycott and also to 'improve the general status of Montgomery, to improve race relations, and to uplift the general tenor of the community'. King was chosen to lead the MIA because he was quite new to Montgomery and the authorities knew little about him. At this stage the demands of the protestors were limited, seeking only to end the policy of black Americans standing when white seats were vacant.

It is thought that about 20,000 people were involved in the Monday boycott. During the evening of 5 December, some 7,000 attended the planned rally and heard Martin Luther King make an inspirational speech.

King was determined to follow the path of non-violence even in the face of police and racist violence. Rosa Parks was fined $10 for the offence on the bus and $4 costs. The MIA then decided to continue the boycott until its demands were met. At this point, the Montgomery authorities made a huge error of judgement. In refusing the moderates' demands, they pushed King and the MIA to demand complete desegregation on buses.

Tasks

1. *Why did the Montgomery Bus Boycott begin in December 1955?*

2. *What can you learn from Source A about the organisers of the boycott? (Remember how to answer this type of question? For further guidance, see page 16.)*

3. *What can you learn from Source B about Martin Luther King? (Remember how to answer this type of question? For further guidance, see page 16.)*

What were the events of the Bus Boycott?

Those boycotting the buses were helped during the first few days by black taxi companies charging only 10 cents per ride. However, within a few days, an obscure Montgomery City Law was used, which stated that the minimum taxi fare had to be 45 cents. Such a figure was too expensive for many black workers. As the boycott progressed, churches bought cars in order to take people to and from work. This created problems because there had to be specific pick-up places for the workers, and while people were waiting they were harassed by the police, who used local laws to try and prevent crowds gathering. The police also attempted to intimidate drivers and arrested many for minor traffic violations. However, the pooling of cars ensured that black Americans continued the boycott.

Source A: **Photograph of Montgomery citizens walking to work during the boycott**

Nevertheless, the boycotters had to face continued intimidation. The Montgomery White Council led the organised opposition. Membership of this body swelled to almost 12,000 by March 1956, and its membership included some of Montgomery's leading city officials. In some cases the violence used against the boycotters was extreme. In January 1956, King's home was firebombed and his wife and young daughter only narrowly escaped injury. Other leaders had their homes firebombed during 1956.

Source B: **Martin Luther King addressing leaders of the boycott. Rosa Parks is seated in the front row and on her right is Ralph Abernathy, a leading figure in the black community.**

Source C: **From Martin Luther King's book *Stride Toward Freedom* (1958). Here he is describing how he addressed the crowd of people who had gathered outside his house, which had been firebombed on 30 January 1956.**

I walked out to the porch and asked the crowd to come to order. In less than a moment there was complete silence. Quietly I told them that I was all right and that my wife and baby were all right. 'Now let's not become panicky,' I continued. 'If you have weapons, take them home; if you do not have them, please do not seek to get them. We cannot solve this problem through retaliatory violence. We must meet violence with non-violence. Remember the words of Jesus: He who lives by the sword will perish by the sword.'

The next step in intimidation came in February 1956, when about 90 of the leading figures – including King and Rosa Parks – were arrested for organising an illegal boycott. Although they were found guilty, no charges were made after appeal.

Success and attempted retribution

As the boycott moved into the summer, the US national press covered events more closely, and this helped raise awareness of the issue of deep racial hatred in the South.

The MIA took the issue of segregation on transport to a federal district court on the basis that it was unconstitutional, citing the Brown v. Topeka case (see page 30). The federal court accepted that segregation was unconstitutional. However, Montgomery city officials appealed and the case went to the Supreme Court. On 13 November 1956, the Supreme Court upheld the federal court's decision. The boycott had been successful. It formally came to an end on 20 December 1956 when King, Abernathy and other leaders travelled on an integrated bus.

The Ku Klux Klan's response was to send carloads of its members around the black areas of Montgomery to try and intimidate the residents. The blacks simply waved at the hooded Klan. In early 1957, there were sniper attacks on some of the buses, King's home was attacked and four churches were bombed, but the white backlash gradually diminished.

Tasks

1. *How useful are Sources A and C as evidence of the Montgomery Bus Boycott? Explain your answer. (For guidance on answering this type of question, see pages 72–73.)*

2. *How did the methods of the opponents of the boycott help King and his followers?*

3. *What can you learn from Source B about those involved in the boycott? (Remember how to answer this type of question? For further guidance, see page 16.)*

4. *Study Source D. Suggest reasons why King was prepared for his supporters to be arrested like Rosa Parks.*

5. *Construct a mind map to show the methods used by King in the boycott.*

6. *Write a newspaper article in support of the boycott.*

What was the role of Martin Luther King?

1929 Born 15 January
1951 Graduated from Crozer Theological College with a degree in theology
1953 Married Coretta Scott
1955 Completed PhD from Boston University
1955 Led Montgomery Bus Boycott
1957 Formed and led Southern Christian Leadership Conference
1963 'I have a dream' speech. Voted 'Man of the year' by *Time* magazine
1964 Winner of the Nobel Peace Prize
1968 4 April, assassinated in Memphis

King was the son of a Baptist minister and grew up in a comfortable middle-class home in Atlanta, Georgia. As a teenager he spoke in his father's church and demonstrated that he had a gift for public oratory. However, he had experienced racial prejudice as a student in such places as Philadelphia, New Jersey and Boston.

Leader of the boycott

He had been minister at the Dexter Avenue Baptist Church, Montgomery, for less than a year when the boycott began. He was chosen as leader of the MIA because of this – he had not been there long enough to grow too close to any particular local organisation. During the dispute he helped to organise the carpools, and when he was prevented from taking out local insurance for the vehicles, he went as far as using Lloyd's of London. His energy and enthusiasm were unbounded in the boycott, and he had the ability to inspire those who worked with him. His idea of using non-violent tactics was similar to the ideas of Gandhi in India, and soon there were many civil rights activists keen to follow King in the quest for equality.

His devout religious beliefs and unwavering faith won him many supporters. He was never intimidated – even when his house was fire-bombed (see page 38). King received several hate letters each day during the boycott, and many of them threatened his life.

> **Source A: From a comment made by King at the end of the boycott**
>
> *We have gained a new sense of dignity and destiny. We have discovered a new and powerful weapon – non-violent resistance.*

Source B: Police photograph of Martin Luther King on his arrest in Montgomery, 22 February 1956

Tasks

1. *Study Source A. How could non-violence be a powerful weapon?*

2. *Study Source B. What impression of Martin Luther King do you gain from this photograph?*

What was the importance of the Bus Boycott?

Following the boycott, King was instrumental in setting up the Southern Christian Leadership Conference, and became its president in 1957. He was now one of the leading figures in the civil rights movement and was a recognisable national figure.

The boycott had shown that unity and solidarity could win, and victory offered hope to those who were fighting for improved civil rights. The NAACP was successful in making a legal case during the boycott and used the Brown case (see page 30) as a precedent. Moreover, the boycott demonstrated the benefits of a peaceful approach and, above all, showed that black Americans were able to organise themselves. It brought King's philosophy to the fore and gave the movement a clear moral framework.

Success also encouraged King to consider further action that would confront inequality and bring about more change.

Source A: From a leaflet written in 1956 by Martin Luther King on the success of the boycott. It was distributed to black Americans involved in the protest.

Remember that this is not a victory for Negroes alone, but for all Montgomery and the South. Do not boast! Do not brag! Be quiet but friendly; proud but not arrogant. Be loving enough to absorb evil and understanding enough to turn an enemy into a friend. If there is violence in word or deed it must not be our people who commit it.

Tasks

1. *Study Source B and use your own knowledge. Why was Source B published? Use details from the photograph and your own knowledge to explain the answer. (Remember how to answer this type of question? For further guidance, see page 34.)*

2. *How useful are Sources A and B as evidence of the success of the Montgomery Bus Boycott? Explain your answer. (For guidance on answering this type of question, see pages 72–73.)*

Source B: A photograph of Rosa Parks (middle) riding at the front of a bus in 1957, after the end of the boycott

Examination practice

This section provides guidance on how to answer the cross-referencing question from Unit 3, which is worth ten marks.

Question 1 – cross-referencing

How far do Sources A and B support the evidence of Source C about the causes of the Montgomery Bus Boycott?

Source A: Adapted from Martin Luther King's speech at Holt Street Baptist Church, 5 December 1955

For many years Negroes in Montgomery have been inflicted with the paralysis of crippling fear on buses. Negroes have been intimidated and humiliated because of the sheer fact that they were Negroes. Just last Thursday, one of the finest citizens in Montgomery was arrested because she refused to get up to give her seat to a white person. Mrs Rosa Parks is a fine person. Nobody can doubt her character. You know my friends there comes a time when people get tired of being trampled over.

How to answer

Use the planning grid on this page to help you organise your answer and the flow chart opposite to show you how to construct your answer.

Source B: From a newspaper article in the *Montgomery Advertiser* **about Martin Luther King's speech at Holt Street Baptist Church, 5 December 1955. It was written by Joe Azbell, a white reporter.**

When the resolution on continuing the boycott of the bus was read, there came a wild whoop of delight. Many said they would never ride the bus again. Negroes turned to each other and compared past incidents on the buses.

At several points there was an emotionalism that the ministers on the platform recognised could get out of control and at various intervals they repeated again and again what 'we are seeking is by peaceful means'.

'There will be no violence or intimidation. We are seeking things in a democratic way and we are using the weapon of protest,' the speakers declared.

Source C: From an article about the Montgomery Bus Boycott on a website created by the *Montgomery Advertiser* **in 2002**

Jo Ann Robinson and lawyer Fred Gray agreed that a long-term legal challenge of bus segregation should be marked by a one-day boycott of the bus system. That evening, after Parks' arrest, Robinson went about setting the boycott into motion. Robinson, who was president of the Women's Political Council, a group of black women who lobbied the city and state on black issues, had been pushing for a bus boycott for months. She saw an opportunity and took it. Later, Robinson said that the Women's Political Council would not wait for Mrs Parks' consent to call for a boycott of city buses.

Source	Details that are similar	Details that differ	Reliability of source	Extent of support
A/C				
B/C				

STEP 1
- Make a note of any parts of Source A that are similar to Source C.
- Now explain any areas of support.

Example:
Source A supports Source C because it suggests that the boycott started after the arrest of Rosa Parks.

STEP 2
- Make a note of any parts of Source A that do not support Source C.
- Now explain any areas of difference.

Example:
Source A suggests it was because black Americans were tired of bad treatment on the buses and just happened, whereas Source C shows it was calculated and planned.

STEP 3
- Make a note of the reliability of Source A.
- Now explain how this supports Source C.

Example:
Source A provides reliable support for Source C because it is the actual speech of Martin Luther King, whose words were recorded at the time.

STEP 4
- Make a note of the unreliability of Source A.
- Now explain how this does not support Source C.

Example:
Source A does not provide reliable support for Source C – King was wanting to win the support of the black Americans in Montgomery and was whipping up the emotions of the crowd.

STEP 5
- Now make a judgement on how much Source A supports Source C.
- Use judgement words or phrases such as 'it strongly supports', 'it provides little support', 'there is some support'.

Example:
Source A gives some support because it suggests that the arrest was crucial and it was an emotional reaction rather than the planned one in Source C.

STEP 6
Now repeat steps 1 to 5 for Source B.

Have a go yourself

STEP 7
Write a conclusion for all three sources. This should begin with the word 'Overall' and make a final judgement on how much Sources A and B support Source C. Remember to use judgement words/phrases.

Have a go yourself

Now have a go yourself

Try answering question 2 using the steps shown for question 1 on page 43.

Question 2 – cross-referencing

How far do Sources A and B support the evidence of Source C about the end of the Montgomery Bus Boycott?

Source A: Adapted from *Race Relations in the USA since 1900*, by V. Sanders, 2000

Montgomery was a limited victory. The victory did not just happen: it was a result of black organisation – the church and the NAACP. It showed the continuing effectiveness of the NAACP strategy of working through the law courts and the importance of dedicated individuals such as Rosa Parks. It demonstrated the importance of the churches in the fight for equality. Above all it brought Martin Luther King to the forefront of the movement.

Source B: From a pamphlet written by Martin Luther King, 19 December 1956

This is a historic week because segregation on buses has now been declared unconstitutional. Within a few days the Supreme Court decision will come into effect and you will be re-boarding integrated buses. This places upon us all a tremendous responsibility of maintaining, in the face of what could be some unpleasantness, a calm and loving dignity befitting good citizens and members of our Race.

Source C: A photograph of Martin Luther King riding a desgregated bus in Montgomery, Alabama, 21 December 1956

Martin Luther King and progress and problems, 1958–62

Source A: **A photograph of a Coca-Cola machine for 'white customers only' in the American South during the 1950s**

DRINK Coca-Cola

ICE COLD

WHITE CUSTOMERS Only!

WHITE CUSTOMERS Only!

6¢

Task

What can you learn from Source A about the American South in the 1950s? (Remember how to answer this type of question? For further guidance, see page 16.)

Though Brown v. Topeka, Montgomery and Little Rock were clear successes in the civil rights movement during the 1950s, there remained much to be done. Many states resented the legislation and, where possible, delayed integration. Moreover, there were many areas in which inequality remained, such as employment opportunities, housing and voting. It seemed as though it would take many years before these inequalities would be eradicated. The years 1958–62 saw some progress, but there was little in the way of legislation to cement any change. However, there were at this time many public protests that prepared the way for the huge developments that occurred after 1963.

This chapter answers the following questions:

- What was the impact of the Civil Rights Act, 1957?
- What part did sit-ins play in civil rights?
- Who were the 'freedom riders'?
- What progress had been made by 1962?

Examination skills

The chapter provides an opportunity to practise some of the question types from Unit 3.

What was the impact of the Civil Rights Act, 1957?

Following the successes of the mid-1950s, **Congress** passed a Civil Rights Act in 1957. It had the support of President Eisenhower, who had always stated that it was impossible to change people's minds by introducing laws. It was hoped that the act would increase the number of black American voters. The act:

- Established the US Commission on Civil Rights. Its first project was to look for evidence of racial discrimination in voting rights in Montgomery, Alabama.
- Emphasised the right of all people to vote, regardless of colour or race.
- Allowed the federal government to intervene if individuals were prevented from voting.
- Stated that all people had the right to serve on juries.

The Crusade for Citizenship

Despite legislation and the raised profile of the civil rights movement, Martin Luther King sought to push for further change. He helped found the Southern Christian Leadership Conference (SCLC) in 1957, following the Montgomery Bus Boycott. The SCLC was black-led and black-run. King and many members of the SCLC felt that boycotts and other forms of non-violent protest should be adopted in the struggle for equality.

The group organised a pilgrimage called the 'Crusade for Citizenship', which marched to the Lincoln Memorial in Washington, DC, in 1957. It also aimed to increase the number of black voters and hoped to force President Eisenhower to speak out on civil rights. The march failed to attract widespread support and Eisenhower refused to be drawn into the debate over civil rights.

> **Source A: From a speech by Martin Luther King Jr to the people of his church, 1959**
>
> *The time has come for a broad, bold advance of the southern campaign for equality. Not only will it include a stepped-up campaign of voter registration, but a full-scale approach will be made upon discrimination and segregation in all forms … We must employ new methods of struggle involving the masses of our people.*

King as civil rights leader

Although King was a visible figure in the civil rights campaign at this time, there were several key events that he did not organise. He responded to this by involving himself wherever there were demonstrations against inequality and as a result he was seen as the leading figure in the civil rights movement by 1963.

Tasks

1. *Why was it significant that the SCLC was 'black-led and black-run'?*

2. *What can you learn from Source A about King's approach to civil rights? (Remember how to answer this type of question? For further guidance, see page 16.)*

What part did sit-ins play in civil rights?

During the late 1950s there were several instances of sit-ins, sit-down demonstrations and boycotts. These were eventually given the term '**direct action**'. The black activist leaders soon realised that direct action often resulted in white violence, which tended to lose support for the whites. The event that pushed the civil rights movement into greater activity came not from organisations like CORE or the NAACP, however, but from students at a college in North Carolina.

Just as King was emerging as a powerful force in the civil rights movement, events in North Carolina showed the lengths to which students would go to fight segregation. A sit-in was held at the Greensboro branch of Woolworths – four black students from a local college demanded to be served at a whites-only lunch counter and, on being refused, remained seated at the counter until the shop closed. The next day, they were accompanied by 27 more students and the day after a further 80 joined them. By the fifth day there were 300. The shop agreed to make a few concessions, but the students later resumed their protests and some were arrested for trespass. The students then boycotted any shop in Greensboro that had segregated lunch counters. Sales immediately dropped and eventually segregation ended. During the sit-ins the students had to endure violence and assaults, but they were careful not to retaliate, copying the tactics Martin Luther King had used at Montgomery. For the second time, the economic weapon and non-violence were used successfully. King visited Greensboro at the height of the sit-in and promised the support of the SCLC.

Consequences of the Greensboro sit-in

- By April 1960, students in 78 communities across the South had held sit-ins.
- 2,000 protestors were arrested.
- By September 1961, it was estimated that there had been about 70,000 black and white students who had used the tactic of the sit-in.
- Variations on a theme developed – there were 'kneel-ins' to integrate churches, 'wade-ins' at beaches, 'read-ins' at libraries and 'sleep-ins' at motel lobbies.
- 810 towns and cities had desegregated public areas by the end of 1961.
- Publicity was gained for the civil rights movement when television showed the non-violence of the protestors in the face of some violent white opponents.
- From all the student upheaval of 1960, there emerged a new pressure group – the Student Non-violent Co-ordinating Committee (SNCC, pronounced 'Snick').

Source A: **A photograph of Greensboro students at the Woolworths counter, 2 February 1960**

Student Non-violent Co-ordinating Committee (SNCC)

The SNCC was founded at Shaw University in Raleigh, North Carolina, in April 1960. It received a grant of $800 from the SCLC to help establish itself. Its first chairman was Nashville college student and political activist Marion Berry. The SNCC, or 'Snick' as it became known, continued its efforts to desegregate lunch counters through non-violent confrontations, but it had only modest success. In May 1961, the group expanded its focus to support local efforts in voter registration as well as public-accommodations desegregation. It played a major role in the key events in the early 1960s – sit-ins, freedom rides, the March on Washington (see page 58) and the 'freedom summer' (see page 66).

(see page 58) ... (see page 66).

Tasks

1. *What is meant by the term 'direct action'?*

2. *Conduct your own research into CORE, NAACP, SCLC and SNCC. Try to find out five additional points about each organisation. (Use the Internet, reference books, and refer also to individuals such as King and Carmichael.)*

3. *Why were the events at Greensboro so important for the civil rights movement?*

4. *Prepare a one-minute talk to explain why you support the method of the sit-in.*

5. *What is paradoxical about Source A (page 47)? Explain your answer carefully.*

6. *What can you learn from Source B about the SNCC? (Remember how to answer this type of question? For further guidance, see page 16.)*

Source B: Badges worn by SNCC members in the 1960s. The badge on the right was the Alabama Christian Movement for Human Rights.

Who were the 'freedom riders'?

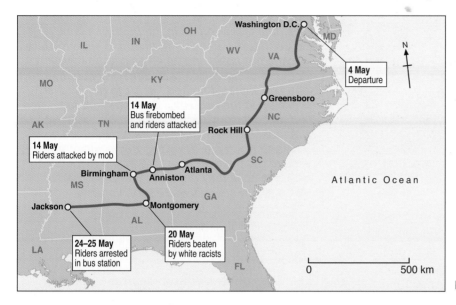

Map of the freedom rides, 1961.

In December 1960, the Supreme Court decided that all bus stations and terminals that served interstate travellers should be integrated. The Congress of Racial Equality (CORE) wanted to test that decision by employing the tactic of the freedom ride. CORE had declined in importance and influence since the late 1950s, and was seeking to revive itself. If there was continued failure to carry out the law, CORE would be able to show that narrow-mindedness and racism still existed in the southern states.

The first of the freedom rides began in May 1961, when James Farmer – the National Director of CORE – and twelve volunteers left Washington, DC, by bus to travel to New Orleans. There was little trouble on the first part of the journey, even when the black Americans used whites-only facilities to ensure integration was taking place. However, in Alabama, one of the buses was firebombed outside Anniston on Mothers' Day – Sunday 14 May 1961. As the bus burned, the mob held the doors shut, intent on burning the riders to death. An exploding fuel tank caused the mob to retreat, allowing the riders to escape the bus, but they were viciously beaten as they tried to

flee. Warning shots fired into the air by highway patrolmen prevented the riders from being lynched on the spot.

In Montgomery, white racists beat up several of the freedom riders. In Jackson, Mississippi, 27 freedom riders from the SNCC and SCLC were jailed for 67 days for sitting in the whites-only section of the bus station. During that year, the membership of CORE doubled, reaching 52,000 by December.

> **Source A: From an interview with James Peck, who rode the first freedom bus. Here he is describing what happened when he arrived in Anniston in May 1961.**
>
> *As Charles Person and I entered the white waiting room and approached the lunch counter, we were grabbed and pushed outside into an alleyway. As soon as we got into the alleyway and were out of sight of the onlookers in the waiting room, six men started swinging at me with fists and pipes. Five others attacked Charles. Within seconds, I was unconscious.*

Reception in Jackson

When the freedom riders reached Birmingham, there was no protection for them and they were attacked by an angry mob – the police chief (Bull Connor) had given most of the police the day off. These events forced the new president, John F. Kennedy, to intervene, and he secured a promise from the state senator in Jackson that there would be no mob violence. However, when the riders arrived in Jackson, they were immediately arrested when they tried to use the whites-only waiting room.

Source C: From an interview with James Zwerg in 1999. Zwerg was talking about his involvement in the freedom rides.

Usually, a white man got picked out for the violence first. I was knocked to the ground. I remember being kicked in the spine and hearing my back crack, and the pain. I fell on my back and a foot came down on my face. The next thing I remember is waking up in the back of a vehicle and John Lewis handing me a rag to wipe my face. I passed out again and when I woke up I was in another moving vehicle with some very southern-sounding whites. I figured I'm off to get lynched. I woke up in the hospital. I was informed that I had been unconscious for a day and a half. A white nurse told me that another little crowd were going to try and lynch me. They had come within a half block of the hospital. She said that she knocked me out in case they did make it, so that I would not be aware of what was happening.

Attacks on the freedom riders

The riders continued throughout the summer, and more than 300 of them were imprisoned in Jackson alone. Attacks on them by the Ku Klux Klan increased. (In 1983, certain **FBI** documents were handed over to the US Justice Department. They revealed that the FBI was aware of the Ku Klux Klan's plans to attack the freedom riders in Birmingham. Moreover, the documents show that one Birmingham police officer told the Klan that no matter how viciously the freedom riders were attacked, there would be no arrests.)

The **attorney general**, Robert Kennedy, did not wish to see the situation escalate and was hoping that he would not have to send in US marshals to

Source D: A photograph of John Lewis (left) and James Zwerg – two freedom riders beaten up by a white mob in Montgomery, Alabama, May 1961

enforce the law. Violence was avoided in Mississippi when it became clear that marshals would be used. On 22 September, the Interstate Commerce Commission issued a regulation that 'prohibited carriers of interstate passengers from having anything whatsoever to do with any terminal facilities which are so operated, arranged, or maintained so as to involve any separation on the basis of race, colour, creed or national origin.'

The freedom rides had been successful. By the early 1960s, there seemed to have been a shift in the composition of people who had been involved in these challenges to the racist system. Now, most were young people and they readily protested that the American claim to have a democracy was a contradiction. They pointed out that the USA's way of life was based on the oppression of black Americans.

Source E: Westbrook Pegler a right-wing journalist writing in the *Jackson Daily News*, 16 June 1961

Today I went to Jackson jail to try to learn from some of the prisoners taken in the miserable fraud called Freedom Riders just what freedom they desired that was denied them. Most of them come from Northern communities where … a white man or woman can go to a public toilet in a bus station without the slightest notice, to say nothing of opposition. So they decided, under organised incitation from offices in New York, to travel a thousand miles to deprive themselves of that freedom and invite personal assault by taunting the people of Jackson. Why had they come to Mississippi – possibly to strike a spark of hatred to light a holocaust in an innocent community of human beings?

Source F: From *The Other American Revolution* by V. Harding

These young people were believers. When they sang in jail, in mass meetings, in front of police and state troopers 'We shall overcome', they meant it … overcoming meant 'freedom' and 'rights' and 'justice' and black and white together … But they knew they were part of a revolution and they believed that if they persisted … they would make it.

Examination practice

Question 1 – Utility

How useful is Source A (page 49) as evidence of the freedom rides? (For guidance on answering this type of question, see pages 72–73.)

Question 2 – Inference

Study Source C. What can you learn from Source C about the attitudes of white people during the freedom rides? (Remember how to answer this type of question? For further guidance, see page 16.)

Question 3 – Cross-referencing

How far do Sources A, B and E agree about the attacks on the freedom riders? (Remember how to answer this type of question? For further guidance, see pages 42–43.)

Question 4 – Source interpretation

Study Source D and use your own knowledge. Why was this photograph taken? Use details from the photograph and your own knowledge to explain your answer. (Remember how to answer this type of question? For further guidance, see page 23.)

Question 5 – Inference

What can you learn from Source F about the changes in the civil rights movement? (Remember how to answer this type of question? For further guidance, see page 16.)

A photograph of protesters demonstrating in Albany during the effort to desegregate the city, 1962.

The Albany Movement, 1961–62

In late 1961, several hundred freedom riders were arrested in Albany, Georgia. Following this, various black groups created the Albany Movement to oppose segregation in the town. Martin Luther King visited Albany and was arrested following a march; he spent a short time in jail because he refused to pay the fine. Despite a concerted effort, the meetings, marches and demonstrations failed to end segregation. Albany's parks and swimming pools were closed, and schools continued to be segregated despite the Brown case and Little Rock. One success was a small increase in the numbers of black Americans who registered to vote, but many in the civil rights movement saw the events at Albany as a failure.

The Voter Education Project

The freedom rides caused Robert Kennedy to fear violent confrontations between the black civil rights groups and white **segregationists**. He felt that if more black Americans voted then they would be able to have a greater say in such issues as housing and education. Kennedy met various groups, and the Voter Education Project was set up in 1962.

The project was staffed mainly by members of the SNCC and they spent much time with eligible voters, showing them how to register and overcome the barriers that were placed in front of them. Following the US Civil War (1861–65) some states prevented black Americans from voting in order to maintain white supremacy. They introduced such things as literacy tests. In Alabama, in order to register to vote, a person had to read out loud to the registrar a section of the constitution (and in some cases verbally interpret it to his satisfaction). Then the applicant had to write out a section of the constitution. After that, there were written questions that were impossible to answer, such as 'How many bubbles in a bar of soap?'

The project resulted in more than 650,000 new registrations, but many people were still refused the right to vote on dubious grounds. SNCC workers were subject to harassment. For example, in Georgia, several churches were bombed, workers were beaten up and some were even shot. Those who did register and voted were sometimes evicted from their land, sacked from their jobs and refused credit. SNCC members felt betrayed because they thought Kennedy would protect them – both President Kennedy and Robert Kennedy were of the opinion that the local police should protect the SNCC workers from the Ku Klux Klan and White Citizens' Councils, but in many cases this did not happen.

In New Orleans, White Citizens' Councils actually bought one-way tickets for black Americans who wished the leave the segregated South and move North.

By the end of 1962, some progress had been made in the campaign for civil rights, but there was still entrenched racism in the South. Moreover, the various civil rights groups had not always agreed among themselves about the best way to proceed. Although King was undoubtedly the leading figure, not enough had been done to raise the issue of civil rights to the top of the domestic agenda in the USA. All this changed in 1963.

Source A: A cartoon in a US newspaper, 1964. The caption was: 'By the way, what's the big word?'

"BY TH' WAY, WHAT'S THAT BIG WORD?"

Tasks

1. *Copy and complete the table below, explaining the reasons why each was successful/unsuccessful.*

	Successful	Unsuccessful
Freedom rides		
The Albany Project		
The Voter Education Project		

2. *Study Source A. What message is this cartoon trying to put across?*

3. *'The civil rights movement made no progress in the years 1958–62'.*
How far do Sources A, B, C, E (pages 49–51) and Source A (left) support this statement? Use the sources and your own knowledge to explain your answer. (For guidance on answering this type of question, see pages 98–100.)

Key Topic 3: Changes in the civil rights movement, 1963–70

Source A: Malcolm X (left) photographing Muhammad Ali, the world heavyweight champion boxer (right). Like Malcolm X, Muhammad Ali was a member of the Nation of Islam and had changed his name from Cassius Clay. The photograph was taken in 1964.

Tasks

1. *Can you suggest reasons why the Nation of Islam was pleased that Source A was published in many papers across the USA?*

2. *Find out what happened to Muhammad Ali when he announced he was a member of the Nation of Islam.*

This key topic examines the **civil rights** movement after 1963, when it gained further momentum. The assassination of President Kennedy in 1963 created a situation whereby the new president, Lyndon B. Johnson, was able to pass two crucial pieces of legislation – the Civil Rights Act (1964) and the Voting Rights Act (1965). Moreover, the civil rights movement, led by Martin Luther King, continued to keep the issues at the forefront of the public's mind with huge marches and demonstrations. Yet during this time, a second – more **militant** – strand grew within the movement. The emergence of figures such as Malcolm X, Stokely Carmichael and Bobby Seale meant that King's non-violent approach was challenged. However, by the end of the 1960s, civil rights was overtaken by the **war in Vietnam** as the USA's most pressing problem.

Each chapter explains a key issue and examines important lines of enquiry as outlined below:

7 Peace marches in 1963

Source A: **From the song 'Only a Pawn in Their Game' written in 1963 by Bob Dylan. This was a song about the murder in that year of Medgar Evers, leader of the NAACP in Mississippi.**

A South politician preaches to the poor white man
'You got more than blacks, don't complain
You're better than them, you been born with white skin' they explain
And the Negro's name is used it is plain
For the politician's gain as he rises to fame
And the poor white remains on the caboose of the train
But it ain't him to blame, he's only a pawn in their game.
The deputy sheriffs, the soldiers, the governors get paid
And the marshals and cops get the same
But the poor white man's used in the hands of them all like a tool
He's taught in his school from the start by the rule
That the laws are with him to protect his white skin
To keep up his hate so he never thinks straight
'Bout the shape that he's in but it ain't him to blame
He's only a pawn in their game.

Tasks

1. *What does Source A show you about racism in the USA in 1963?*

2. *What does the title of the song mean?*

The 1960s saw tremendous gains for black Americans. Suddenly, it seemed as if the issue of civil rights could no longer be ignored. The profile was raised by a number of marches that gained worldwide publicity. It was these marches that brought Martin Luther King to worldwide prominence and led to the legislation of the mid-1960s.

This chapter answers the following questions:

• Why was the Birmingham March of 1963 so important?
• Why was the March on Washington so important?

Examination skills
In this chapter you will be given further guidance on how to answer the cross-referencing question, which is worth ten marks.

Why was the Birmingham March of 1963 so important?

The civil rights issue seemed to explode in 1963. Although the **sit-ins** had enjoyed some success, there was still no federal law that made southern states integrate their public facilities. In order to avoid **desegregating** its parks, playgrounds, swimming pools and golf courses, the city of Birmingham, Alabama, simply closed them all. The Southern Christian Leadership Conference (SCLC) sought to challenge the city with Project C – 'Confrontation' – which would use the tactics of sit-ins and marches to press for desegregation at lunch counters. It was hoped that the demonstrations would achieve maximum publicity across the USA. Birmingham had a population of about 350,000, of which about 150,000 were black Americans. King hoped to mobilise a large part of them in the planned demonstrations.

The demonstrations began on 3 April 1963, and on 6 April some activists were arrested. Police Chief Eugene 'Bull' Connor closed all public parks and playgrounds. This prompted King to address a large rally, at which he said it was better to go to jail in dignity rather than just accept **segregation**. King was arrested in a further demonstration on 12 April and jailed for defying a ban on marches. He was arrested on Good Friday and during his short stay in prison, he wrote 'Letter from Birmingham Jail' (see Source C). This letter became one of the most famous documents of the civil rights movement, and many see it as one of the most powerful in history.

The situation worsened on his release from jail on 20 April. It was decided that children and students would be used in the demonstrations, and this seemed to change the methods used by

> Source A: **Police dogs attacking civil rights demonstrators in Birmingham, Alabama, 3 May 1963**

the police. On 3 May, Police Chief Connor allowed his men to set dogs on the protesters, and then called in the fire department to use powerful water hoses. Connor placed almost 2,000 demonstrators in jail. Around 1,300 children were arrested and there was concern about students missing school. Television witnessed the events, and these images were seen not only across the USA but all over the world. Photographs of the demonstration and police reaction were published in national newspapers. This gave King all the publicity he wanted. It showed the violence of the authorities in the face of peaceful demonstrators. By 3 May there was chaos in Birmingham.

It was at this stage that President Kennedy became involved – he sent Assistant **Attorney General** Burke Marshall to mediate between the parties in the hope of finding a solution. Desegregation was eventually introduced in the city. A consequence of the violence was Kennedy's decision to bring in a Civil Rights Bill (see Source D). Talks between King and the Birmingham city leaders brought a settlement by 9 May, and it was agreed that desegregation would take place in the city within 90 days.

On that same day, 11 June 1963, Medgar Evers, leader of the Mississippi National Association for the Advancement of Colored People, was shot dead in Jackson by a white sniper.

Source B: Fire hoses being turned on demonstrators in Birmingham, 3 May 1963. The hoses were powerful enough to rip the bark off trees, loosen bricks from walls and knock people down.

Source C: Part of King's 'Letter from Birmingham Jail'

Our direct-action program could be delayed no longer. Non-violent direct action seeks to create a crisis and foster such a tension that a community which has constantly refused to negotiate is forced to confront the issue … For years, I have heard the word 'Wait!' It rings in the ear of every Negro with piercing familiarity. This 'Wait!' has almost always meant 'Never'. We must come to see that justice too long delayed is justice denied. The nations of Asia and Africa are moving with jet-like speed toward gaining political independence, but we still creep at horse and buggy pace toward gaining a cup of coffee at a lunch counter.

Source D: From a speech made on television by President Kennedy on 11 June 1963, about the need to improve civil rights for black Americans

We preach freedom around the world, and we mean it … But are we to say to the world – and much more importantly to one another – that this is the land of the free except for the Negroes? We face a moral crisis as a country and a people. It cannot be met by repressive police action. It cannot be left to increased demonstrations in our streets. It is a time to act in Congress and in our daily lives.

Tasks

1. How useful are Sources A and B as evidence of the tactics used by the police in Birmingham in 1963? Explain your answer. (For guidance on answering this type of question, see pages 72–73.)

2. Why did King choose Birmingham to demonstrate?

3. What can you learn from Source C about King's changing attitude? (Remember how to answer this type of question? For further guidance, see page 16.)

4. Why did President Kennedy become so involved in the crisis at Birmingham?

5. Study Source D. What did President Kennedy mean when he said 'We face a moral crisis'?

Why was the March on Washington so important?

Source A: A photograph of Bayard Rustin and Cleveland Robinson, two of the organisers of the March on Washington

After Birmingham, the civil rights groups wanted to maintain the impetus and some sought to commemorate the centenary of the freeing of the slaves in 1863. The idea of a huge march on Washington, DC, was put forward by Philip Randolph, who had suggested a similar march in 1941. Randolph was given close assistance by Bayard Rustin and Cleveland Robinson. The key groups of NAACP, **CORE**, **SNCC** and SCLC took part in organising the march. King was keen to have the march because he knew that there were those in the movement who felt that progress was slow and who might drift towards violence if the high profile was not sustained. Indeed, the Washington police halted leave for its 3,000 officers and called on the services of 1,000 police officers from neighbouring locations in case there was violence. There were also 2,000 members of the National Guard on standby. President Kennedy also feared violence at the march and he asked the organisers to call it off.

The march initially began as a cry for jobs and freedom, but its aims broadened to cover those of the whole of the civil rights movement. There was naturally a demand for the passage of Kennedy's Civil Rights Bill.

The rally at Washington

When the march took place, there were about 250,000 demonstrators (it has been estimated that there were around 80,000 white supporters) – the organisers had expected less than half this figure. People came from all over the USA – by plane, train, bus and car. When **senators** and congressmen were seen, there were chants of 'Pass the bill' (meaning Kennedy's Civil Rights Bill). Before the speakers, Bob Dylan sang several songs, one of which was 'Only a Pawn in Their Game' (see page 55) and he was joined by other protest singers.

Photograph of Martin Luther King at the Lincoln Memorial, August 1963.

Not all the speakers were moderate in their approach. John Lewis of the SNCC was forced to amend his speech, but even so, the one he delivered was very powerful (see Source B).

'I have a dream'

King was the final speaker of the day and his speech has now become part of the lore of the struggle for civil rights (see Source C). He used his skill as an orator and included many biblical references, which appealed to all sections in society.

Although there were some detractors – Malcolm X (see pages 76–77) called it a 'farce on Washington' – the March on Washington was hailed as a great success. It was televised across the USA and did much for the civil rights movement. It brought together different sections of US society and put further pressure on President Kennedy to move on civil rights.

Effects of the march

After the march, King and the other leaders met President Kennedy to discuss civil rights legislation. Kennedy was keen to let them know of his own commitment to the Civil Rights Bill. However, all those at the meeting were aware that there were many **Republican** politicians still opposed to any changes. No opposition politician in the **Senate** changed his mind about Kennedy's Civil Rights Bill

King's hopes seemed illusory because in September 1963, four black girls were killed in a bomb attack while attending Sunday school in Birmingham. Violence erupted on the day of the bombing and two black youths were killed in the aftermath. The movement seemed to stall in late 1963 and was then hit by the assassination of President Kennedy.

Tasks

1. *Study Source A. What did the organisers mean by the word 'freedom'?*

2. *Why was it important for the civil rights movement to have the support of famous actors and protest singers?*

3. *Working in pairs, put forward a list of reasons why the March on Washington was a success.*

4. *Study Sources B and C. In what ways is Lewis different to King in his view of civil rights?*

5. *Can you suggest reasons why King's speech (Source C) has become one of the most famous in history?*

Examination practice

This section provides further guidance on how to answer the cross-referencing question from Unit 3, which is worth ten marks.

Question 1 – cross-referencing

How far do Sources A, B and C support the view that black Americans had to be patient in their demands for improved civil rights? Explain your answer.

> ### Source A: From the speech made by John Lewis, radical member of the SNCC, at the March on Washington, 28 August 1963
>
> *The revolution is at hand, and we must free ourselves of the chains of political and economic slavery. For those who have said, 'Be patient and wait!' we must say, 'Patience is a dirty and nasty word.' We cannot be patient, we do not want to be free gradually, we want our freedom, and we want it now. We cannot depend on any political party, for the Democrats and the Republicans have betrayed the basic principles of the Declaration of Independence.*

> ### Source B: From an article in *The New York Post*, 29 August 1963
>
> *Probably the greatest public relations triumph was provided by the marchers themselves. Their dignity, good humour, patience and pleasant sincerity created an image which the American white can grasp. The white may not identify with the bitter rock-throwers in Birmingham or battered students in Montgomery. But he can understand the plight of a portly 40-year-old Negro with a wife and three children who wants to stay in the best motel he can afford.*

> ### Source C: Walter Reuther, president of the United Auto Workers Union, speaking at the March on Washington, 28 August 1963
>
> *For 100 years the Negro people have searched for first-class citizenship and I believe that they cannot and should not wait until some distant tomorrow. They should demand freedom now. Here and now. It is the responsibility of every American to share the impatience of the Negro American. And we need to join together, to march together, and to work together until we have bridged the moral gap between American democracy's noble promises and its ugly practices in the field of civil rights.*

How to answer

Use the planning grid on this page to help you to organise your answer and the flow chart opposite to show you how to construct your answer.

Source	Details that support the view	Details that differ	Reliability of source	Extent of support
A				
B				
C				

STEP 1
- Make a note of any parts of Source A that support the view.
- Now explain any areas of support.

Example:
Source A supports the view because it suggests that there are people who are saying that black Americans should be patient. Political parties appear to expect patience.

STEP 2
- Make a note of any parts of Source A that do not support the view.
- Now explain any areas of difference.

Example:
Source A shows how Lewis rejects the idea of patience and demands immediate change which should be brought about by black Americans.

STEP 3
- Make a note of the reliability of Source A.
- Now explain how this supports the view.

Example:
Source A provides reliable support for the view because it is from Lewis' speech at the meeting, listened to by thousands of people.

STEP 4
- Make a note of the unreliability of Source A.
- Now explain how this does not support the view.

Example:
Source A does not provide reliable support for the view because Lewis was a radical member of the SNCC and he wanted to arouse the passions of the audience.

STEP 5
Now make a judgement on how much Source A supports the view. Use judgement words or phrases such as 'it strongly supports', 'it provides little support', 'there is some support'.

Example:
Source A gives only basic support for the view because it suggests that he is tired of the attitude of those who have been patient, and he and some black Americans are no longer prepared to act in a similar manner.

STEP 6
Now have a go yourself for Sources B and C by repeating steps 1 to 5 for each source.

Have a go yourself

STEP 7
Write a conclusion for all three sources. This should begin with the word 'Overall' and make a final judgement on how much the three sources support the view. Remember to use judgement words/phrases.

Have a go yourself

Now have a go yourself

Try answering question 2 using the steps shown for question 1 on page 61.

Question 2 — cross-referencing

How far do Sources A, B and C support the view that it was the police who were responsible for the trouble in Birmingham in 1963? Explain your answer.

Source A: **Police leading black schoolchildren into jail following their arrest for protesting against racial discrimination near Birmingham City Hall, 4 May 1963**

Source B: **From *Free at Last?* by F. Powledge, 1991**

Shortly after the settlement of 9 May, the Ku Klux Klan held a rally on the edge of town. Afterward, during the night, an explosion ripped through the Gaston Hotel where Martin Luther King had been staying. An estimated 2,500 black Americans poured out of their homes and into the streets. Some of them rioted, setting police cars on fire and breaking department store windows and looting. In some cases white motorists were dragged from their cars and beaten up.

Source C: **From *Race, Reform and Rebellion* by M. Marable, 1991**

On 2 May 1963, a children's march was organised. It involved 6,000 black youngsters from the ages 6 to 16. Before national television cameras, Birmingham police let loose vicious police dogs on children as they knelt to pray. 959 children were arrested. Police used firehoses and clubs against women, children and the elderly.

8 Martin Luther King and civil rights legislation

Source A: From the Nobel Peace Prize citation for Martin Luther King, 1964

He is the first person in the Western world to have shown us that a struggle can be waged without violence. He is the first to make the message of brotherly love a reality in the course of his struggle, and he has brought this message to all men, to all nations and races. We pay tribute to Martin Luther King, the man who has never abandoned his faith in the unarmed struggle he is waging, who has suffered for his faith, who has been imprisoned on many occasions, whose home has been subject to bomb attacks, whose life and the lives of his family have been threatened, and who nevertheless has never faltered.

Task

What can you learn from Source A about the character of Martin Luther King? (Remember how to answer this type of question? For further guidance, see page 16)

The mid-1960s saw the passing of the two most important pieces of legislation of the whole civil rights era – the Civil Rights Act (1964) and the Voting Rights Act (1965). However, the passage of these two acts did not come easy. The Civil Rights Act followed on from dreadful events in Birmingham (see page 56) and the assassination of President Kennedy. The Voting Rights Act came after yet more deaths, marches and demonstrations in Alabama. In 1968, Martin Luther King was assassinated and many US cities experienced riots in black areas, clearly showing the continued dissatisfaction black Americans felt about their lives.

This chapter will answer the following questions:

• What role did President Kennedy play in civil rights?
• What was the 'Freedom Summer'?
• Why was the Civil Rights Act of 1964 important?
• Why did voting rights become an issue in 1965?
• What was the impact of King's assassination?

Examination skills
In this chapter you will be given guidance on how to answer the utility question, which is worth ten marks.

What role did President Kennedy play in civil rights?

Source A: A letter from the leader of the NAACP to President Kennedy, January 1961

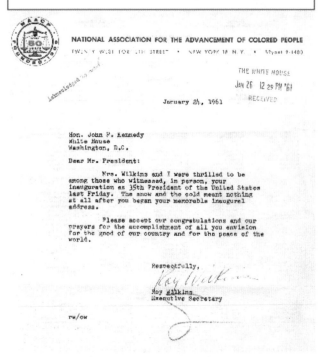

NATIONAL ASSOCIATION FOR THE ADVANCEMENT OF COLORED PEOPLE
TWENTY WEST FORTIETH STREET • NEW YORK 18 N.Y. • BRyant 9-1400

THE WHITE HOUSE
Jan 26 12 29 PM '61
RECEIVED

January 24, 1961

Hon. John F. Kennedy
White House
Washington, D.C.

Dear Mr. President:

Mrs. Wilkins and I were thrilled to be among those who witnessed, in person, your inauguration as 35th President of the United States last Friday. The snow and the cold meant nothing at all after you began your memorable inaugural address.

Please accept our congratulations and our prayers for the accomplishment of all you envision for the good of our country and for the peace of the world.

Respectfully,

Roy Wilkins,
Executive Secretary

rw/ow

Task

1. *Study Source A. Suggest reasons why the NAACP sent such a letter to President Kennedy.*

During the 1960 presidential election campaign, Kennedy ensured that he campaigned in urban areas where there were heavy concentrations of black voters. Kennedy was instrumental in securing the release of Martin Luther King from jail in Atlanta (see page 56), an act that won him some support.

When one considers the narrow margin of Kennedy's victory (out of 68 million votes cast, Kennedy won by 112,827 votes), winning the black vote had been crucial. In his **inauguration speech**, President Kennedy put forward the idea of the **New Frontier**. One part of this was to achieve equality for black Americans. However, he had to be very astute in his approach because he faced opposition not only from his own party (the **Dixiecrats**, see page 29) but also **white supremacists** across the USA.

Kennedy was aware that he had to accept King and his methods. During the Birmingham riots in 1963 (see page 56), Robert Kennedy echoed his brother's views when he said:

> *'If King loses, worse leaders are going to take his place.'*

Source B: From a speech by President Kennedy after the University of Alabama was desegregated in 1963

It is as old as the scriptures and is as clear as the American Constitution. The heart of the question is whether all Americans are to be afforded equal rights and equal opportunities, whether we are going to treat our fellow Americans as we want to be treated. If an American, because his skin is dark, cannot eat lunch in a restaurant open to the public, if he cannot send his children to the best school available, if he cannot vote for the public officials who represent him, if, in short, he cannot enjoy the full and free life which all of us want, then who among us would be content to have the colour of his skin changed and stand in his place? Who among us would then be content with the counsels of patience and delay?

During his time as president, Kennedy:

- Appointed five black federal judges, including Thurgood Marshall. Marshall was a leading civil rights activist and his appointment showed Kennedy's commitment to this issue.
- Appointed his brother (Robert) as Attorney General. This meant that law courts could be used to ensure that civil rights laws were not circumvented.

- Appointed other black Americans to his administration, such as Carl Rowan (Deputy Assistant Secretary of State), Robert Weaver (Director of the Housing and Home Finance Agency), Mercer Cook (Ambassador to Norway), George Weaver (Assistant Secretary of Labour).
- Threatened legal action against the state of Louisiana for refusing to fund schools that were not segregated.
- Sent 23,000 government troops to ensure that just one black student, James Meredith, could study at the University of Mississippi (see page 33).
- Threatened to evict the Washington Redskins football team from their stadium, which was funded by the **federal government**, unless they agreed to hire black players.
- Introduced a Civil Rights Bill to **Congress** in February 1963. This aimed to give black people equality in public housing and education. This decision won him many supporters among black Americans.

A photograph of the leaders of the Washington March meeting President Kennedy, 28 August 1963. King is second on the left and Kennedy is the fourth from right.

Tasks

2. *Why was the black vote crucial to President Kennedy?*

3. *What did Robert Kennedy mean when he said 'If King loses, worse leaders are going to take his place.' Explain your answer.*

4. *Study Source B.*
a) *What problems facing black Americans does President Kennedy highlight?*
b) *What does he imply in the last sentence?*

5. *Choose the three achievements of President Kennedy that you think are most important. Explain your choices.*

However, Kennedy's achievements were limited. He did not play a leading role in the civil rights movement for fear of losing the support of southern **Democrats**, who opposed civil rights, and he only stepped in with firm commitments after events in Birmingham (see page 56).

What was the 'Freedom Summer'?

A photograph of students having a lesson in a Freedom School, Mississippi, 1964.

The Mississippi Freedom Party

Kennedy's Civil Rights Bill went through its first stages in November 1963, but his assassination delayed its progress. After the high point of the Washington March and now the delay in passing the Bill, the civil rights movement organised the 'Freedom Summer'. CORE, the SNCC and the NAACP acted together in this, with the aim of increasing the number of registered voters in Mississippi. Mississippi had the lowest number of registered voters of blacks in the USA (around seven per cent). Black Americans were prevented from voting by being forced to take extremely difficult literacy tests (see page 53) in order to register. They often suffered arson attacks, beatings and even **lynchings** if they attempted to register.

The three groups formed the Mississippi Freedom Party (MFDP), and more than 80,000 people joined it. They established 30 Freedom Schools in towns throughout Mississippi in order to address the racial inequalities in Mississippi's educational system. Volunteers from across the USA taught in the schools. The curriculum included black history and the philosophy of the civil rights movement. It has been estimated that more than 3,000 students attended these schools that summer and almost 70,000 by the end of the year.

The schools and volunteers became the target of white racists, and there were bombings and assaults – sometimes by the police. More than 30 churches were bombed. However, the 'Freedom Summer' became notorious because of the murder of three of the project's volunteers – James Chaney and his two white colleagues, Andrew Goodman and Michael Schwerner.

Chaney, Goodman and Schwerner

On 21 June, Chaney, Goodman and Schwerner were arrested while they were investigating a church bombing. They were taken in for traffic offences that day by a policeman who was a member of the **Ku Klux Klan**. They were held for several hours, but were eventually released from police custody. They were never seen again. The police officer had informed his associates in the Klan of the arrests and they began to plan the murders.

Six weeks later, three badly decomposed bodies were discovered under a nearby dam. Goodman and Schwerner had been shot in the chest and Chaney had been severely beaten and shot. (The film *Mississippi Burning*, starring Gene Hackman and Willem Dafoe, is about this incident.)

Once again, the civil rights movement gained support and President Johnson was firm in his resolve to find the murderers. It was ironic that on 2 July, at the height of this crisis, President Johnson signed the Civil Rights Act (see page 68).

There were some resulting issues for the black members of the movement, who claimed that there was such nationwide publicity only because two of the victims were white. At the end of the 'Freedom Summer', some activists returned home and turned their attention to different causes. Others, such as Stokely Carmichael, began to look at more radical approaches to bringing about change. Nevertheless, most of those involved in the summer's protests saw their actions as successful when, in 1965, the Voting Rights Act was passed (see page 69).

Source A: An FBI poster raising awareness of the missing Goodman, Chaney and Schwerner, August 1964

Tasks

1. *Why was Mississippi chosen as the focus of the 1964 demonstrations?*

2. *Study Source A and use your own knowledge. Why was the poster published? Use details from the poster and your own knowledge to explain the answer. (Remember how to answer this type of question? For further guidance, see page 23.)*

3. *What were the results of the 'Freedom Summer'?*

Why was the Civil Rights Act of 1964 important?

A photograph of President Johnson signing the Civil Rights Act on 2 July 1964. Martin Luther King is standing behind him.

Following the death of President Kennedy, his successor, Lyndon B. Johnson, was able to push the Civil Rights Bill through the House of Representatives and the Senate, ensuring that those southern Democrats who opposed the bill would be counterbalanced by Republicans. Johnson had been in high-level politics since 1938 but he needed all his skills to persuade and cajole the Republicans to vote with him. He had put forward his vision of a 'Great Society', which would attack racial injustice and poverty. This was in the same spirit as Kennedy's 'New Frontier'. There was deep shock within the USA at Kennedy's assassination, and there were some in Congress who voted sympathetically for the bill. Johnson also won some support in Congress because he was a southerner, from Texas.

The Civil Rights Act is seen as President Johnson's greatest achievement. However, there were many black Americans who criticised it as being insufficient and coming rather late in the day. Naturally, there were many white Americans in the South who resented it and sought to make it fail.

The Civil Rights Act, 1964

- Segregation in hotels, motels, restaurants, lunch counters and theatres was banned.
- The Act placed the responsibility on the federal government to bring cases to court where **discrimination** still occurred.
- Any business engaged in transactions with the government would be monitored to ensure there was no discrimination.
- The Fair Employment Practices Committee, which had been set up during the Second World War (see page 27), was established on a permanent basis.
- The Act created the Equal Employment Opportunity Commission (EEOC) to implement the law.

Tasks

1. *How could both black and white Americans criticise the 1964 Civil Rights Act?*

2. *Write a newspaper article praising the passing of the Civil Rights Act. Write a headline for your article of about six words.*

Why did voting rights become an issue in 1965?

Voting Rights

In 1870, by the Fifteenth Amendment, male black Americans were given the right to vote. However, some states **disenfranchised** them by such means as unfair taxation and literacy tests. The literacy tests were not a test of reading and writing – they asked difficult arithmetic and cultural questions that most people would have found impossible (see page 53).

The Civil Rights Act did not mean that black Americans could vote, so King and his colleagues decided to force the issue by embarking on another non-violent campaign. The town of Selma, Alabama, was to be the battleground, as only 383 black Americans out of 15,000 had been able to register as voters. The sheriff of Selma, Jim Clark, had a reputation which matched that of Bull Connor in Birmingham (see page 56). King was hoping for a brutal reaction to his demonstrations because he knew that the press and television would again highlight the continued bigotry of the South.

There were two months of attempts to register black voters – and two months of rejections. King and his followers were subjected to beatings and arrests. One demonstrator was murdered.

It was decided to hold a march from Selma to the state capital, Birmingham, in order to present to Governor Wallace a petition asking for voting rights. Governor Wallace banned the march but King was determined to take his supporters and lobby him.

The march was stopped on the Edmund Pettus Bridge and the marchers were attacked by Sheriff Clark's men and state troopers. The marchers faced tear gas, horses and clubs, and were forced to return to Selma. This became known as 'Bloody Sunday' and the event forced President Johnson's hand. A second march took place two days later but King turned the marchers back – he had agreed with Johnson that he would avoid another violent confrontation with Clark.

Source A: A photograph of the civil rights march to the Edmund Pettus Bridge, Selma, 1965

Public opinion across the USA was firmly behind King and the civil rights movement, and on 15 March, President Johnson promised to put forward a bill that would **enfranchise** black Americans. Eventually, it was agreed that a march from Selma to Montgomery would go ahead if it was peaceful. On 21 March, King led more than 25,000 people – the biggest march ever seen in the South.

Tasks

1. *What can you learn from Source A about the civil rights march from Selma? (Remember how to answer this type of question? For guidance, see page 16.)*

2. *Was King justified in putting the lives of his followers at risk in the Selma marches? Explain your answer.*

The Voting Rights Act, 1965

The success of the march created an atmosphere of optimism and in the summer, President Johnson introduced the Voting Rights Bill. This Act:

• ended literacy tests
• ensured federal agents could monitor registration – and step in if it was felt there was discrimination. It was presumed that if less than 50 per cent of all its voting-age citizens were registered then racial discrimination was being exercised.

By the end of 1965, 250,000 black Americans had registered (one-third had been assisted by government monitors, who checked that the law was being followed). A further 750,000 registered by the end of 1968. Furthermore, the number of elected black representatives increased rapidly after the bill was enacted.

King's policy of non-violence appeared to have worked. There was widespread support and sympathy from white Americans, and there had been two key pieces of legislation that had removed discrimination and disenfranchisement.

However, other groups were emerging that opposed King's idea of non-violence. There was a feeling among some that progress was slow and that, too often, King had been ready to make deals with the white authorities. These groups will be explored in Chapter 9.

During the next three years, King remained at the forefront of the civil rights movement, and in 1966 he focused his efforts on helping black Americans in the North by means of a major campaign in Chicago. In 1968, he became involved in the Poor People's Campaign. However, he did lose the support of some Americans when he began to criticise US involvement in the Vietnam War.

Tasks

3. *What can you learn from Source B about voters in the USA in 1969? (Remember how to answer this type of question? For further guidance, see page 16.)*

4. *Re-read the sections on the Civil Rights Act (page 68) and the Voting Rights Act. Which do you think was the more important? Explain your answer.*

Source B: Table showing registered voters in certain states in the USA, 1969

State	Percentage of white people registered	Percentage of black people registered
Alabama	94.6	61.3
Arkansas	81.6	77.9
Florida	94.2	67.0
Georgia	88.5	60.4
Louisiana	87.1	60.8
Mississippi	89.8	66.5
North Carolina	78.4	53.7
South Carolina	71.5	54.6
Tennessee	92.0	92.1
Texas	61.8	73.1
Virginia	78.7	58.9
USA as a whole	80.4	64.8

What was the impact of King's assassination?

On 4 April 1968, Martin Luther King was visiting Memphis in support of black refuse collectors, who were striking for equal treatment with their white co-workers. This was an indication that social and economic issues were becoming increasingly important to the civil rights movement.

The economic and educational gulf between blacks and whites was still great, not only in the South but also in the North. However, King was finding it increasingly difficult to control his followers, who struggled with his principle of non-violence. King was assassinated that day in Memphis. James Earl Ray, a white racist, was arrested and jailed for the crime, but there is still doubt over whether he was the real killer.

On King's death, there was a final outburst of rioting across the country. Forty-six people died, more than 3,000 were injured in violent clashes, and there were demonstrations in more than 100 cities. This violence was a great irony – it seemed as if King's whole work and life had been for nothing.

The year 1968 seemed to mark the end of an era. There was a new president, Richard Nixon, the Vietnam War had begun to dominate the domestic scene and the student movement also took centre stage.

In 1983, President Reagan established Martin Luther King Day as a national holiday, to be held on the third Monday in January.

Tasks

1. *Study Source A. What did King mean when he said 'We as a people will get to the Promised Land'?*

2. *Can you suggest reasons why there was rioting across the USA on the death of Martin Luther King?*

A photograph of the Ebenezer Baptist Church, Atlanta, where King's funeral was held on 11 April 1968. About 100,000 people came for the service, though the church would only hold 800. After the funeral, a mule-drawn wagon carried King's body through Atlanta's streets to Morehouse College, followed by up to 200,000 mourners.

Examination practice

This section provides guidance on how to answer the utility question from Unit 3, which is worth ten marks.

In answering the utility question, you must analyse various aspects of two sources and, in order to reach the top level, you need to cover them all. The content and nature, origin and purpose (NOP) of a source should be considered, and out of this there will emerge an evaluation of the source's utility and reliability.

In order to reach higher-level marks for this question you have to explain the value (usefulness) and limitations of both the content and the NOP of each source. The NOP is found in the provenance of the source – the information given above or below it. A good tip is to highlight or underline key words in the provenance that show either the utility or limitations of the source. An example of this approach is given for Source A on page 73.

There is also guidance in the box below of what to consider for the NOP of a source.

NOP means...

N Nature of the source
What type of source is it? A speech, a photograph, a cartoon, a letter, an extract from a diary? How will the nature of the source affect its utility. For example, a private letter is often very useful because the person who wrote it generally gives their honest views.

O Origins of the source
Who wrote or produced the source? Are their views worth knowing? Are they giving a one-sided view? When was it produced? It could be an eyewitness account. What are the advantages and disadvantages of eyewitness accounts?

P Purpose of the source
For what reason was the source produced? For example the purpose of adverts is to make you buy the products. People usually make speeches to get your support. How will this affect the utility of the source?

Question 1 – utility

How useful is Source A as evidence of the 'Freedom Summer'? Explain your answer.

How to answer

Although in the exam the question will be on two sources, in question 1 we look at one source to help you build your skill in analysing a source. Question 2 on page 74 is about two sources.

First let us concentrate on content. For each source you should think about the following questions:

1. What is useful about the content of the source?
- What does it mention? How useful is this compared to your own knowledge of the event? This is known as your contextual knowledge.
- What view does it give about the feelings of people? Given your contextual knowledge, how typical is this view of the time. For example:

> Source A gives the view that the voter registration drive was part of a communist plot. This is useful because it is typical of the 'Red Scare' tactics of those that opposed civil rights.

2. Are there any limitations to the content? For example:
- Does it give a very limited or one-sided view?
- What does it not tell us about the event or person? For example:

> Source A is of limited use because it gives a one-sided view of the registration drive by those that opposed black registration. Moreover, it provides no evidence of those that supported the movement.

Now let's move on to NOP. Page 73 shows examples of the value and limitations of the NOP of Source A as evidence of the 'Freedom Summer'.

Nature

This suggests it is useful because it is a newspaper that would have been read by many people and prepared for a distinct readership, thus giving us details about actual events.

Origins

This makes it less reliable and useful because it was an article written by opponents of the civil rights movement who would want to give a damning view of the 'Freedom Summer'.

Purpose

This is useful because it is an example of right-wing propaganda which tries to play on the fear of communism in the USA. This is useful because it helps us to understands why there was opposition to the 'Freedom Summer'.

Nature

This is of limited use because it is a newspaper article and may not be accurate or typical of newspapers across the USA. Hence, one point of view fails to present us with a broad view of the 'Freedom Summer'.

Origins

This makes it useful because it was published during the 'Freedom Summer' and gives one view of events at the time.

Purpose

The article has deliberately given a very critical and exaggerated picture in order to increase resentment towards the civil rights movement, which makes it less reliable and useful.

> **Source A:** An editorial about the 'Freedom Summer' from the *Lowell Liberator* a right-wing US newspaper June, 1964
>
> *This newspaper a long time ago pointed out that a part of the Communist plan in the United States is to stir up racial strife. The ultimate aim is a black revolution. A thousand college students from the North are reported to be invading Mississippi this summer in order to engage in a Negro voter registration drive. It is unbelievable that a thousand college students would do this of their own volition. Those who know the ways of propaganda, correctly suspect that the idealism of some college youngsters has been taken advantage of by Communists who want to stir up trouble in the South.*

Now have a go yourself

Answer question 1 using all the guidance given on these two pages. Make a copy of the planning grid below and use it to plan your answer. If you need further guidance on how to analyse the value and limitations of the contents of a source, look back to page 60.

PLANNING GRID		
	Value	**Limitations/unreliability**
Contents		
What does the source tell you?		
What view does the source give?		
NOP		
Nature		
Origin		
Purpose		

The utility of two sources

For Edexcel Unit 3 you will need to evaluate the utility of two sources.

Question 2 – utility

How useful are Sources B and C as evidence of those involved in the 'Freedom Summer'? Explain your answer.

How to answer

- Explain the value and limitations/reliability of the contents of each source.
- Explain the value and limitations/reliability of the NOP of each source.
- In your conclusion give a final judgement on the relative value of each source. For example, one source might provide one view of an event, the other source a different view.

Make a copy of the grid on page 73 to plan your answer for each source.

Below is a writing frame to help you.

Make a copy of the grid on page 73 to plan your answer for each source.

Source B: From an application to join CORE's 'Freedom Summer' project in 1964

Since I have become active in CORE here in New York, I have become increasingly aware of the problems which exist in the Southern states. I wish to become an active participant rather than a passive onlooker. As a teacher I have been working in South Jamaica, Queens, where I not only have had experience in dealing with teenagers, but have become increasingly concerned with the conditions under which these children must live. My hope is to someday pass on to the children we may have a world containing more respect for the dignity and worth of all men that that would which was willed to us.

Source C: From an article about the 'Freedom Summer' in the *Dallas Morning News*, July 1964

The President should now use the force of his office to attack the cause of the trouble in Mississippi. That trouble is the unjustified, uncalled for invasion of that sovereign state by a bunch of Northern students schooled in advance in causing trouble under the guise of bringing 'freedom' to Mississippi Negroes. The invasion of these young busybodies therefore was planned far in advance and, incredibly, has the support of the National Council of Churches. The students were schooled in invasion at Western College for Women in Oxford, Ohio.

So there you have it. An 'invasion' planned in advance with the announced strategy of creating trouble.

Source C is useful because (contents) it suggests...

Moreover, Source C is also useful because of (NOP)..

Source C has limitations/unreliable including (contents)..

Source C is also of limited use/unreliable because (NOP)..

Source D is useful because (contents) it suggests..

Moreover, Source D is also useful because of (NOP)..

Source D has limitations/unreliable including (contents)..

Source D is also of limited use/unreliable because (NOP)..

In conclusion, Sources C and D are useful because they...

9 Malcolm X and Black Power

Source A: Malcolm X, speaking in 1963 about the March on Washington

Yes I was there. I observed that circus. Who ever heard of angry revolutionists all harmonising 'We shall overcome ... Suum Day ...' while tripping and swaying along arm-in-arm with the very people they were supposed to be angrily revolting against? Who ever heard of angry revolutionists swinging their bare feet together with their oppressor in lily-pad park pools, with gospels and guitars and 'I have a dream' speeches? And the black masses in America were – and still are – having a nightmare.

Task

Study Source A. What was Malcolm X's attitude towards the March on Washington?

The 1960s was a strange and paradoxical decade for the civil rights movement. There was support from presidents Kennedy and Johnson. Legislation such as the Civil Rights Act (see page 68) and the Voting Rights Act (see page 69) removed the major areas of discrimination. Moreover, Martin Luther King had raised the profile of the injustices that black Americans had to endure. On the other hand, though, the USA saw its worst racial violence and rioting during the years 1965–67. It also saw the rise of militant leaders such as Malcolm X, Bobby Seale and Huey Newton, and the formation of the paramilitary Black Panthers. And, by the end of the decade, the issue of civil rights had been overtaken by the war in Vietnam.

This chapter answers the following questions:

• What role did Malcolm X play in the civil rights movement?
• What was Black Power?
• What was the Black Panther movement?
• Had progress been made by the end of the 1960s?

Examination skills

The chapter provides an opportunity to practise some of the question types from Unit 3.

What role did Malcolm X play in the civil rights movement?

For some in the civil rights movement, progress had been painfully slow, and a feeling grew that King's methods would never bring equality either in politics or in opportunities in life. A group that had never accepted King's ideas was the **Nation of Islam** (or Black Muslims) – its supporters openly sought **separatism**. Members rejected their slave surnames and called themselves 'X'.

The most famous member of the Nation of Islam was Malcolm X, and his brilliant oratorical skills helped increase membership of the group to about 100,000 in the years 1952–64. He was a superb organiser and during his membership of the Nation of Islam, he travelled across the USA winning converts. Malcolm X helped set up educational and social programmes aimed at black youths in **ghettoes**. By 1960, more than 75 per cent of members of the Nation of Islam were aged 17–35. Malcolm X is credited with re-connecting black Americans with their African heritage and is responsible for the spread of Islam in the black community in the United States. His influence on people such as Carmichael (see page 79) was crucial.

Biography Malcolm X (Malcolm Little), 1925–65

1925 Born 19 May in Omaha
1931 Father murdered by white supremacists.
1942 Lived in New York, involved in pimping and drug dealing
1946 Found guilty of burglary and imprisoned
1952 Released from jail. Had become a follower of the Nation of Islam. Changed his name to 'X'.
1958 Married Betty Shabazz
1964 Left the Nation of Islam and formed Muslim Mosque, Inc. and the black nationalist Organization of Afro-American Unity
1964 Went on pilgrimage to Mecca. His political and religious views altered. Changed his name to Malik El-Hajj Shabazz.
1965 21 February, shot by three members of the Nation of Islam

---

Source B: From Malcolm X's autobiography, written in 1964 with the help of Alex Haley, a prominent black American writer, and published after Malcolm X's death. The book appealed to militant blacks and by 1970 had sold more than four million copies in the USA.

Every time you see a white man, think about the devil you're seeing! Think of how it was on your slave ancestors' bloody sweaty backs that he built his empire that's today the richest of all nations – where his evil and his greed cause him to be hated around the world.

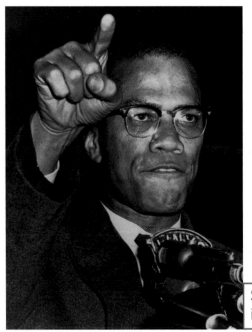

Source A: Malcolm X addressing a rally on 14 May 1963, in support of desegregation in Birmingham, Alabama

Many members of the mainstream civil rights groups did not like the Nation of Islam, and some felt that the Muslims had a 'hate-white doctrine', which was as dangerous as any white racist group. Thurgood Marshall (see page 64) said that the Nation of Islam was run by a 'bunch of thugs organised from prisons and financed by some Arab group'. Such criticism did not concern Malcolm X and he was never afraid to attack King and other leaders of the civil rights movement. He criticised the 1963 March on Washington, which he called 'the farce on Washington'. He could not understand why so many black people were impressed by 'a demonstration run by whites in front of a statue of a president who has been dead for a hundred years and who didn't like us when he was alive'.

> ## Source C: From a speech by Malcolm X in New York, 12 December 1964
>
> *I believe in the brotherhood of man, all men, but I don't believe in brotherhood with anybody who doesn't want brotherhood with me. I believe in treating people right, but I'm not going to waste my time trying to treat somebody right who doesn't know how to return the treatment.*

Malcolm X had a tremendous influence on young urban black Americans. He felt that violence could be justified not only for self-defence but also as a means to secure a separate black nation. However, after a visit to Mecca, he changed his views and left the Black Muslims to set up the Muslim Mosque Inc. and the Organization of Afro-American Unity to promote closer ties between Africans and African-Americans. Malcolm X said the trip to Mecca allowed him to see Muslims of different races interacting as equals. He came to believe that Islam could be the means by which racial problems could be overcome. He pushed to end racial discrimination in the USA, but this brought him enemies, and he was assassinated by three black Muslims in February 1965.

Malcolm X's views and ideas became the foundation of the more radical movements such as Black Power (see page 78) and the Black Panthers (see page 81). Many historians have said that Malcolm X helped raise the self-esteem of black Americans more than any other individual in the civil rights movement.

> ## Source D: From Malcolm X's speech at the Founding Rally of the Organization of Afro-American Unity, 28 June 1964
>
> *We have formed an organization known as the Organization of Afro-American Unity, which has the same aim and objective to fight whoever gets in our way, to bring about the complete independence of people of African descent here in the Western Hemisphere, and first here in the United States, and bring about the freedom of these people by any means necessary. That's our motto. We want freedom by any means necessary. We want justice by any means necessary. We want equality by any means necessary.*

> ## Source E: From Malcolm X's funeral oration, given by the black American actor Ossie Davis
>
> *Many will ask what Harlem finds to honour in this stormy, controversial and bold young captain – and we will smile. They will say he is of hate – a fanatic, a racist … and we will answer 'Did you ever talk to Brother Malcolm? Did you ever really listen to him? Did he ever do a mean thing? Was he ever associated with violence or any public disturbance?' … in honouring him, we honour the best in ourselves.*

> ## Tasks
>
> 1. *Study Source A. How does Malcolm X come across in this photograph?*
>
> 2. *Why was it important for the Nation of Islam to offer educational and social programmes?*
>
> 3. *To whom was Malcolm X referring when he said '… a president who has been dead for a hundred years'?*
>
> 4. *Does Source D support Sources B and C about Malcolm X's attitude to racism?*
> *(Remember how to answer this type of question? For further guidance, see pages 60–61.)*
>
> 5. *How reliable is Source E about Malcolm X? Explain your answer using the sources and your own knowledge.*

What was Black Power?

Despite the Civil Rights Acts (1957 and 1964 – see page 68), many young black Americans were frustrated, and those who lived in the ghettoes felt anger at the high rates of unemployment, continuing discrimination and poverty they experienced. On 11 August 1965, this frustration exploded into a major riot in the Watts district of Los Angeles. The riot left 34 dead, 1,072 injured, 4,000 arrested and caused about $40 million of damage.

There were riots across the USA's major cities in the two following summers. Many followed a similar pattern – the arrest of a black youth, a police raid, rumours of police brutality and then the explosion of the riot. Huge numbers of rioters were involved – 30,000 in the Watts riot. Racial violence peaked in the summer of 1967, when there were race riots in 125 US cities. The two largest occurred less than two weeks apart in July: Newark left 26 dead and over 1,000 injured, and Detroit resulted in more than 40 dead, hundreds injured and 7,000 arrested.

During the three summers of riots, more than 130 people were killed and the damage totalled more than $700 million.

Source B: **Looters being arrested after the riots in Newark, 1967**

Source A: **Police facing rioters, Detroit, 1967**

Tasks

1. *What can you learn from Source A about the riot in Detroit? (Remember how to answer this type of question? For further guidance, see page 16.)*

2. *Study Source B. Can you suggest reasons why leaders of the civil rights movement condemned the looting?*

3. *What is meant by the term 'Black Power'?*

4. *What can you learn from Source C about Stokely Carmichael? (Remember how to answer this type of question? For further guidance, see page 16)*

The emergence of Black Power

As the riots raged, the Black Power movement emerged. This was originally a political slogan but in the late 1960s it came to cover a wide range of activities that aimed to increase the power of blacks in American life. Stokely Carmichael and others in the SNCC wanted blacks to take responsibility for their own lives and rejected white help. For some black activists, Black Power meant separatism, but for others it was a way of ridding the USA of a corrupt power structure. Carmichael and his associates wanted black Americans to create their own political force so that they would not have to rely on the black groupings that existed at the time.

Carmichael and his followers wanted blacks to have pride in their heritage. They promoted African forms of dress and appearance, and adopted the slogan 'Black is beautiful'.

Carmichael attracted criticism because of his aggressive attitude, and was attacked when he denounced the involvement of the USA in the Vietnam War. He eventually left the SNCC and became associated with the Black Panthers, but left the USA and moved to Guinea in 1969, where he lived until his death in 1998.

Stokely Carmichael, leader of the SNCC.

Biography Stokely Carmichael, 1941–98

1941	Born in Port of Spain, Trinidad and Tobago
1943	Moved to New York City
1960	Attended Howard University, Washington, DC. Gained a degree in Philosophy.
1961	Took part in the freedom rides, jailed for seven weeks
1966	Chairman of the SNCC
1966	Twenty-seventh arrest – made his 'Black Power' speech
1967	Wrote *Black Power*
1968	Joined Black Panthers
1969	Left the USA, moved to Guinea. Changed his name to Kwame Ture.
1998	Died in Guinea

Source C: From a speech made in 1966 by Stokely Carmichael, leader of the Student Non-violent Co-ordinating Committee, describing his own frustrations and those of many black Americans. He had just been released from police custody following involvement in a civil rights march in Mississippi.

This is the twenty-seventh time I have been arrested. I ain't going to jail no more. The only way we gonna stop them white men from whuppin' us is to take over. We been saying freedom for six years and we aint got nothin'. What we gonna start sayin' now is Black Power!

The 1968 Olympics

The Black Power movement gained tremendous publicity at the 1968 Mexico Olympics, at the winners' ceremony for the men's 200m and 400m relay. The athletes wore part of the movement's uniform – a single black glove and a black beret – and also gave the clenched-fist salute. During the ceremony, when the US national anthem was being played, Smith gave the salute with his right hand to indicate Black Power and Carlos with his left to show black unity. Smith also wore a black scarf to represent black pride, and black socks with no shoes to represent black poverty in racist America. Their action created such a furore that, following the ceremony, Smith and Carlos were banned from the athlete's village and sent back to the USA. They were accused of bringing politics into sport and damaging the Olympic spirit. On their return, they both received several death threats. As a result of this sporting event, the whole world became aware of the Black Power movement.

Source E: **The US 400 metres relay team at the 1968 Olympic Games, giving the Black Power salute and wearing the movement's black berets**

Source D: **Tommie Smith and John Carlos at the 1968 Olympic Games. Smith won the gold and Carlos the bronze in the 200 metres.**

Tasks

5. *Write a speech for an SNCC meeting. In it explain why you have now rejected King's approach and agree with the ideas of Stokely Carmichael.*

6. *How useful are Sources D and E as evidence of the Black Power movement? (Remember how to answer this type of question? For further guidance, see pages 72–73.)*

7. *Working in groups, prepare either a case to support or condemn the US athletes at the Mexico Olympics in 1968.*

What was the Black Panther movement?

Source A: **A photograph of Bobby Seale (left) and Huey Newton, co-founders of the Black Panther Party for Self Defence**

At the same time as the urban riots and the development of 'Black Power', there emerged the 'Black Panthers'. This party was founded by Huey Newton and Bobby Seale in October 1966 in Oakland, California. Both of these men had been heavily influenced by Malcolm X.

Eldridge Cleaver, the party's Minister of Information, wrote *Soul on Ice* (1967), setting out the aims of the Panthers in a ten-point programme. The Black Panthers were prepared to use revolutionary means to achieve these aims. They were even prepared to form alliances with radical white groups if they felt it would help bring down the 'establishment'. The leaders of the Panthers advocated an end to **capitalism** and the establishment of a socialist society. Seale constantly stated: 'We believe our fight is a class struggle and not a race struggle.'

Tasks

1. *What can you learn from Source A about the Black Panthers? (Remember how to answer this type of question? For further guidance, see page 16.)*

2. *Study Source B. Which of these aims do you think that Martin Luther King would have opposed?*

Source B: **The Black Panthers' ten-point programme, October 1966**

We want:
1. *Freedom. We want power to determine the destiny of our Black Community.*
2. *We want full employment for our people.*
3. *We want an end to the robbery by the white man of our Black Community.*
4. *We want decent housing, fit for shelter of human beings.*
5. *We want education for our people that exposes the true nature of this decadent American society. We want education that teaches us our true history and our role in the present-day society.*
6. *We want all black men to be exempt from military service.*
7. *We want an immediate end to police brutality and murder of black people.*
8. *We want freedom for all black men held in federal, state, county and city prisons and jails.*
9. *We want all black people when brought to trial to be tried in court by a jury of their peer group or people from their black communities, as defined by the Constitution of the United States.*
10. *We want land, bread, housing, education, clothing, justice and peace.*

Source C: From *Revolutionary Suicide* (1973) by Huey Newton

We had seen Watts rise up the previous year. We had seen how the police attacked the Watts community after causing the trouble in the first place. We had seen Martin Luther King come to Watts in an effort to calm the people, and we had seen his philosophy of non-violence rejected. Black people had been taught non-violence; it was deep in us.

What good, however, was non-violence when the police were determined to rule by force? We had seen all this, and we recognized that the rising consciousness of Black people was almost at the point of explosion. Out of this need sprang the Black Panther Party. Bobby Seale and I finally had no choice but to form an organisation that would involve the lower-class brothers.

Source E: J. Edgar Hoover, FBI Director, quoted in the *New York Times*, 9 September 1968

The Black Panthers are greatest threat to the internal security of the country. Schooled in communist ideology and the teaching of Chinese Communist leader Mao Tse-tung, its members have perpetrated numerous assaults on police officers and have engaged in violent confrontations with police throughout the country. Leaders and representatives of the Black Panther Party travel extensively all over the United States preaching their gospel of hate and violence not only to ghetto residents, but to students in colleges, universities and high schools as well.

The Panthers wore uniforms and were ready to use weapons, training members in their use. By the end of 1968, they had 5,000 members. However, internal divisions and the events of 1969 – which saw 27 Panthers killed and 700 injured in confrontations with the police – resulted in diminishing support. The group was constantly targeted by the **FBI** and by 1982 the Black Panthers had disbanded.

Source D: The symbol of the Black Panther Party

POWER TO THE PEOPLE

Tasks

3. *How useful are Sources B (page 81) and C in helping you understand the attraction of the Black Panthers? (Remember how to answer this type of question? For further guidance, see pages 72–73.)*

4. *What image does source D project of the Black Panthers?*

5. *Study Source E. Why do you think that the FBI closely monitored the Black Panthers?*

6. *'The Black Power Movement and the Black Panthers were a threat to the security of US society in the 1960s.'*
How far do Source B (page 78), Source C (page 79), and Sources A, B and E (pages 81–82) support this statement? Use details from the sources and your own knowledge to explain your answer. (For guidance on how to answer this type of question, see pages 98–100.)

Had progress been made by the end of the 1960s?

The riots of 1965–67 caused President Johnson and his advisers to look into the factors behind them. The Black Power movement had made it clear that equality of opportunity did not exist and the Kerner Report (1968) stated that racism was deeply embedded in American society. This report not only highlighted the economic issues faced by black Americans, but also the 'systematic police bias and brutality'. The Kerner Report recommended sweeping federal initiatives that would mean increased expenditure. Following the election of President Nixon later that year, the report was largely ignored.

The year did seem to be the end of an era, with the election of a new president, the ongoing Vietnam War and the rise of the student movement. However, there had been significant changes, and the legislation of the 1960s had given equality and protection before the law. Despite this, the riots of 1965–67 and those that occurred on the death of Martin Luther King in 1968 indicated that there was still huge frustration among the black population.

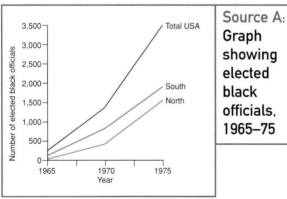

Source A: Graph showing elected black officials, 1965–75

Source B: From an article about civil rights in a British history magazine for GCSE students

There were definite improvements in the quality of life for many of America's disadvantaged; in 1965, 19 per cent of black Americans earned the average wage, by 1967, this had risen to 27 per cent; in 1960, the average educated age of a black American was 10.8, by 1967 this had increased to 12.2.

Source C: Black American and national unemployment figures in the years 1960–70

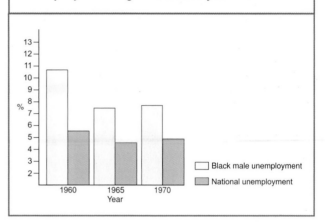

Source D: A table showing the percentage of people living in poverty in the USA in the years 1959–68

	1959	1963	1966	1968
Whole population	22.4	19.5	14.7	12.8
Whites	18.1	15.3	11.3	10.0
Non-whites	56.2	51.0	39.8	33.5

Task

'By 1970, black Americans had made positive gains in the struggle for civil rights.' How far do Source A (page 81) and Sources A–D (this page) support this statement? Use details from the sources and your own knowledge to explain the answer. (For guidance on answering this type of question, see pages 98–100.)

Key Topic 4: Other protest movements in the 1960s

Source A: Students burning their draft cards (call-up to the armed forces) in 1968

GIRLS SAY YES to boys who say NO

Proceeds from the sale of this poster go to The Draft Resistance.

Source B: A poster of 1968 about the war in Vietnam: Say NO to war!

Tasks

1. *What can you learn from Source A about the student protest movement of the 1960s? (Remember how to answer this type of question? For further guidance, see page 16.)*

2. *What is the purpose of Source B? (Remember how to answer this type of question? For further guidance, see page 23.)*

This key topic examines protest in the USA in the 1960s, including the student and women's movements. It explains the reasons for the student movement, especially the influence of the 'Swinging Sixties' and the **war in Vietnam**, and the key features of that movement and its influence on American society. In addition, it examines the position of women in the USA in the early 1960s, and the attempts by various women's groups and individuals, such as Betty Friedan, to change that position.

Each chapter explains a key issue and examines important lines of enquiry as outlined below:

Chapter 10 Reasons for student protest (pages 85–90)

- Why did the student movement emerge?
- What was the importance of the conflict in Vietnam?

Chapter 11 Key features of the student movement (pages 91–100)

- How did the students campaign?
- Why was the student movement important?

Chapter 12 The women's movement (pages 101–112)

- What was the impact of the Second World War?
- How did the women's movement emerge?
- What did the women's movement achieve?
- How did the women's movement develop?
- What links were there between the protest movements?

Reasons for student protest

Source A: From the Bob Dylan song 'Blowin' in the Wind'

How many times must a man look up
Before he can see the sky?
Yes, 'n' how many ears must
one man have
Before he can hear people cry?
Yes, 'n' how many deaths will it take
till he knows
That too many people have died?
The answer, my friend,
is blowin' in the wind,
The answer is blowin' in the wind.

Task

What is the message of the song?
Pick out words and phrases to illustrate
this message.

Bob Dylan in 1965.

There were several reasons for the emergence of the student protest movement of the 1960s. It was partly inspired by the culture of the 'Swinging Sixties' and protest singers such as Bob Dylan. In addition it was influenced by key personalities such as Martin Luther King and John F. Kennedy. However, much opposition was directed at US involvement in the conflict in Vietnam.

This chapter answers the following questions:

• Why did the student movement emerge?
• What was the importance of the conflict in Vietnam?

Examination skills

In this chapter you will be given guidance on how to answer the reliability question, which is worth ten marks.

Why did the student movement emerge?

Many students took a leading role in protest movements during the 1960s. This had a particularly significant impact on attitudes to the US involvement in the war in Vietnam. So why did the student movement emerge?

The legacy of the 1950s

The 1950s was a decade of frustration and anger for many young Americans. They wanted to rebel against everything, especially what their parents believed. This frustration led to heavy drinking and the formation of teenage gangs. The media seemed to fuel this rebellious attitude. Films such as *Rebel without a Cause*, featuring James Dean, led the way, followed by the emergence of rock 'n' roll, a new type of music that spread across the USA and Europe. Parents hated it, which made it even more attractive to teenagers. Elvis Presley was also very influential, with his tight jeans and gyrating stage act.

The 'Swinging Sixties'

The attitudes of teenagers in the 1950s carried over to the next decade. It is often described as the 'Swinging Sixties', as the young distanced themselves even more from the older generation and its view of how they should behave. Young people demanded greater freedom in everything they did: the music they listened to, the clothes they wore, the social life they led. This greater freedom, in turn, was influenced by the introduction of the contraceptive pill, which gave women much more choice over whether and when to have children. It also led to greater freedom in sexual behaviour and the wider use of recreational drugs.

Source B: **Mario Savio, a Berkeley student, explaining his opposition to traditional US society, 1964**

There is a time when the operation of the machine becomes so odious, makes you so sick at heart, that you can't take part; you can't even passively take part and you've got to put your bodies upon the gears and upon the wheels, upon the levers, upon all apparatus and you've got to make it stop.

A photograph of Mario Savio at a demonstration against the war in Vietnam, 1966.

Universities

Many students wanted a greater say in their own education. They wanted to take part in running the universities and an end to college rules and restrictions. In addition, student societies tried to expose racism in their own colleges. Starting in 1964, a wave of strikes and demonstrations affected nearly every university and college in the country. Some tried to ban the protests and the students responded with a 'free speech' campaign. Nearly half of Berkeley's 27,500 students took part in this campaign in 1964 and 1965.

Protest singers

The 1960s saw an explosion in pop music that was both an expression of this emerging **youth culture**, and of protest against important issues of the day. On page 85 there is a verse from Bob Dylan's protest song, 'Blowin' in the Wind'. The lyrics to this and many of his other songs covered the themes of the changing times: nuclear war, racism and the hypocrisy of waging war.

The British invasion by pop groups including the Beatles and the Rolling Stones challenged the music scene. The songs were about peace, free love and drugs. Artists such as Jimi Hendrix, Janis Joplin and Joan Baez sang about sex, drugs and opposition to the war in Vietnam.

The death of Kennedy

Kennedy's **New Frontier** policies (see page 64) sought to harness the youth of America to his reform programme and captured the imagination and support of many. His assassination in 1963 angered and disillusioned many young Americans and drove them into protest movements.

The influence of Martin Luther King

For many young Americans – white and black – their first experience of protest was in **civil rights**. Martin Luther King's methods proved inspirational and many white students supported the freedom marches, freedom rides (see page 49) and the **sit-ins** of the early and mid-1960s.

The worldwide phenomena

The 1960s were also a time of student protest across the world. For example, in the later 1960s there were student protests in Northern Ireland in support of civil rights for Catholics, and in 1968 student demonstrations in Paris were so serious they almost overthrew the government.

Biography Bob Dylan, b. 1941

He was born Robert Allen Zimmerman in 1941, the grandchild of Jewish-Russian immigrants. Robert started writing poems at the age of ten and taught himself basic piano and guitar in his early teens. He was heavily influenced by contemporary rock stars such as Elvis Presley and Jerry Lee Lewis.

In 1959, he moved to Minneapolis and attended the University of Minnesota where he became even more interested in music and began performing solo at local nightspots, adopting the name of Bob Dylan. He soon dropped out of college and began writing his own songs, establishing himself with songs such as 'Blowin' in the Wind' and 'Like a Rolling Stone'. He was important for two main reasons:

- He brought poetry into mainstream rock music.
- Many of his songs attacked the injustice and intolerance of American society. He became a symbol of change.

Tasks

1. *What can you learn from Source B about the reasons for the student movement? (Remember how to answer this type of question? For further guidance, see page 16)*

2. *How useful is Source A as evidence of the reasons for the student movement?*

3. *Look again at the extract from Dylan's protest song on page 85. Now see if you can write at least one verse of your own protest song. You could set it to your favourite type of music.*

What was the importance of the conflict in Vietnam?

Vietnam had been split by civil war. The **communists** governed North Vietnam whilst the government in the south was strongly anti-communist. The USA did not want communist North Vietnam to take over the South.

Under presidents Kennedy and Johnson, the USA became increasingly involved in the conflict in Vietnam. They were committed to defending South Vietnam from a takeover by the communist North Vietnamese, whose guerrilla forces – known as the Vietcong – were gaining increasing support from the peasants in the south. Indeed, Johnson actually declared war on the North in 1964 and sent a great number of US troops to fight in Vietnam. Direct US involvement lasted until 1973 when, under President Nixon, American troops were withdrawn.

US involvement in the war in Vietnam divided US society, especially as the casualty list mounted and the media highlighted US atrocities against Vietnamese civilians. On the other hand, opposition to the war united the student movement. Half a

million young Americans were fighting in the war and many others would be called up by the **draft** or **conscription** system.

Reasons for opposition to the war

1. Many students were called up to the armed forces. This was known as the draft system.
2. Opposition to the war grew with the number of casualties. In 1965 there were fewer than 2,000 US casualties. By 1968 that number had increased to 14,000.
3. Some students questioned the right of the USA to be in Vietnam. The USA was supporting a corrupt regime in South Vietnam.
4. US methods of warfare brought even greater opposition, especially against the use of chemical weapons such as napalm and the killing of innocent civilians such as the massacre at My Lai.
5. The media did much to whip up student opposition. The war in Vietnam was the first to be televised in great detail. Colour television, readily accessible by the late 1960s, worsened the bloody nature of what was shown.

Source A: A photograph that appeared in a US newspaper, showing an anti-war demonstration in front of the Pentagon in October 1967

Tasks

1. *How useful is Source A as evidence of the opposition of students in the USA to the war in Vietnam?*

2. *The reasons for student protest can be linked to each other. Do your own concept map with reasons for student protest as the central box and boxes leading off with each reason.*
   - *Rank order the reasons clockwise from the most to the least important.*
   - *Use different coloured pens to show links between some of the reasons.*
   - *Briefly explain the link between the reasons.*

Examination practice

This section provides guidance on how to answer the reliability question from Unit 3, which is worth ten marks.

Question 1 – reliability

How reliable are Sources A and B as evidence the student movement of the 1960s? Explain your answer.

How to answer

You are being asked whether you can trust what the source is suggesting.

- Compare what the source suggests to your own contextual knowledge. In other words, what you know about the person or event.
- Examine the nature, origins and purpose (NOP) of the source with reference to reliability.
- Cross-reference the two sources to see if they support each other.

A reminder of what to consider for NOP is on page 72. On page 90 is an example of how you could approach this for Source A.

A reminder of what to consider for NOP is on page 72. On page 90 is an example of how you could approach this for Source A.

> ### Source A: From a speech made by a student at the Fifth Peace Parade Committee, 1967
>
> *We demand that no more American youth be sent to fight in a war that is helping neither them nor the Vietnamese people. We have learned lessons from Nazi Germany and will not go along with the aggressive war-making policies of any government, even if it happens to be our own.*

Source B: A poster issued by the Berkeley Free Speech Movement in 1968

Nature
Less reliable because this is a speech intended to encourage people to support the peace movement.

Origins
Reliable because it is by a student who is giving the views of the peace movement at that time.

Purpose
Less reliable because it is trying to turn people against the peace movement.

> **Source A:** From a speech made by a student at the Fifth Peace Parade Committee, 1967
>
> *We demand that no more American youth be sent to fight in a war that is helping neither them nor the Vietnamese people. We have learned lessons from Nazi Germany and will not go along with the aggressive war-making policies of any government even if it happens to be our own.*

Purpose
Reliable because it provides the views of the peace movement.

Contextual knowledge
Reliable because US tactics, especially the use of napalm and the murder of innocent civilians, were not helping the people of South Vietnam.

Source B: A poster issued by the Berkeley Free Speech Movement in 1968

Cross-referencing
Reliable because the anti-war views of Source A are supported by those of Source B.

Now have a go yourself with Source B. Make a copy of the planning grid below and use this to plan your answer

Source	Reliable	Unreliable
Contextual knowledge		
Nature		
Origins		
Purpose		
Cross-referencing		

Key features of the student movement

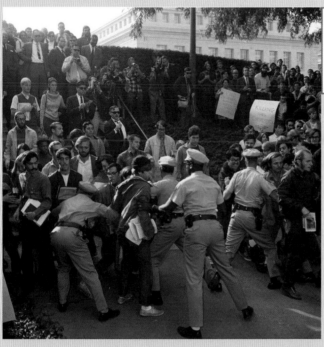

Source A: **A photograph of a student demonstration at the University of California, Berkeley, in December 1967**

Task

Devise two captions for the photograph in Source A:
• *one from the student movement*
• *one by the government.*

Students were heavily involved in the civil rights movement, in organisations such as the **SNCC** and **CORE** and, by the mid-1960s, they were ready to use this experience to campaign for greater rights for themselves as well as to oppose the war in Vietnam. The leading student organisation was Students for a Democratic Society (SDS), which was first noticed nationally when it organised a sit-in at the University of California, Berkeley, in 1964. The anti-war campaign culminated in the death of four people during a demonstration at Kent State University, Ohio, in 1970. During the second half of the 1960s, many young people demonstrated in a different way by becoming part of the hippy movement.

This chapter answers the following questions:

• How did the students campaign?
• Why was the student movement important?

Examination skills

In this chapter you will be given guidance on how to answer the hypothesis testing question, which is worth sixteen marks.

How did the students campaign?

The student movement began in the early 1960s with a demand for a greater say in how courses and universities were run, but it gathered increasing support and momentum due to opposition to the war in Vietnam.

Involvement with civil rights

In 1964, student societies organised rallies and marches to support the civil rights campaign. Many were appalled at the racism in American society and were determined to expose racists in their own colleges, and demanded 'free speech'.

The SDS

One of the first student protest groups to emerge in the USA was the Students for a Democratic Society (SDS). It was set up in 1959 by University of Michigan student Tom Hayden, to give students a greater say in how courses and universities were run. The SDS denounced the Cold War and adopted a position of 'anti-anti-Communism', demanding controlled disarmament to avoid the possibility of a nuclear war. The SDS also wanted to help the poor and disadvantaged. It eventually formed groups in 150 colleges and universities, and had 100,000 members by the end of the 1960s. Its support increased after President Johnson announced bombing raids on North Vietnam in 1965.

It first achieved national prominence when, in 1964, it organised a sit-in against a ban on political activities at the University of California at Berkeley. This was followed by a series of similar sit-ins across the USA. Membership greatly increased when, in 1966, President Johnson abolished student draft deferments, which had allowed some men to delay their call-up for the armed forces. Three hundred new SDS branches were set up.

The SDS organised a variety of activities against the war in Vietnam, including staging draft-card burnings, harassing campus recruiters for the CIA, occupying buildings in universities and destroying draft-card records.

Source A: A statement issued by the SDS in 1962

Universal controlled disarmament must replace deterrence and arms control as the [American] national defense goal ... It is necessary that America make disarmament, not nuclear deterrence, 'credible' to the Soviets and to the world. That is, disarmament should be continually avowed as a national goal; concrete plans should be presented at conference tables.

Source B: A BBC news report, October 1967

The biggest demonstration yet against American involvement in the Vietnam War has taken place in the town of Oakland, in California. An estimated 4,000 people poured onto the streets to demonstrate in a fifth day of massive protests against the conscription of soldiers to serve in the war. The city was brought to a standstill as protesters built barricades across roads to prevent buses carrying recruits to the army's conscription centre. Police reinforcements came in from San Francisco as the protests turned violent. Demonstrators, many wearing helmets and holding plywood shields, overturned cars and threw bottles, tin cans and stones at the police. Four people were injured and seven arrested.

Source C: Student protestors stage a sit-in at Columbia University, New York, April 1968

At the 1968 Democratic Convention in Chicago, SDS protestors – organised by Tom Hayden – created a riot in order to destroy the election chances of the pro-war candidate, Hubert Humphrey. Hayden and six others were arrested and convicted of crossing state lines to incite a riot. They became known as the Chicago Seven.

Tasks

1. *What can you learn from Source A about the early aims of the SDS? (Remember how to answer this type of question? For further guidance, see page 16.)*

2. *How useful is Source B as evidence of the student movement?*

3. *What message are the students trying to put across in Source C?*

Opposition to the war in Vietnam

Opposition to the Vietnam War united the student movement. Such opposition arose due to the increasing US death toll and the tactics employed by the US, including mass bombing, the use of chemical weapons and the killing of many Vietnamese civilians. Moreover, a disproportionate number of black American students were called up to fight in Vietnam. Influential black figures such as Martin Luther King spoke out against the war.

The anti-war protests reached their peak during 1968–70. In the first half of 1968, there were over 100 demonstrations against the war, involving 400,000 students. In 1969, 700,000 marched in Washington, DC, against the war. Students at these demonstrations often burned draft cards or, more seriously, the US flag, which was a criminal offence. This in turn led to angry clashes with the police.

The worst incident occurred at Kent State University, Ohio, in 1970. Students were holding a peaceful protest against President Nixon's decision to bomb Cambodia as part of the Vietnam War. Moreover, many were incensed by a speech he made in May 1970 (see Source C).

National Guardsmen, called to disperse the students, used tear gas to try to move them. When they refused to move shots were fired. Four people were killed and eleven injured (see Source E). The press in the USA and abroad were horrified, and some 400 colleges were closed as two million students went on strike in protest against this action.

A few days later two students at another university who were protesting against the killings at Kent State University were shot dead by police.

Source C: Part of Nixon's speech, 1 May 1970

You think of those kids out there (in Vietnam). They are the greatest. You see these bums blowing up the campuses … they are the luckiest people in the world, going to the greatest universities and here they are burning up the books, I mean storming around about – get rid of the war. Out there [in Vietnam] we've got kids who are just doing their duty. They stand tall and they are proud.

Source D: A student demonstration against the war, 1968

Source E: One of the students killed at Kent State University in 1970

Source F: Arthur Krause, the father of one of the students who died at Kent State University, talking about his daughter on TV, 5 May 1970

She resented being called a bum because she disagreed with someone else's opinion. She felt that our crossing into Cambodia was wrong. Is this dissent a crime? Is this a reason for killing her? Have we come to such a state in this country that a young girl has to be shot because she disagrees deeply with the action of her government?

Source G: From the memoirs of Richard Nixon, written in 1978

Those few days after Kent State were among the darkest of my presidency. I felt utterly dejected when I read that the father of one of the dead girls had told a reporter: 'My child was not a bum.'

Tasks

4. *Study Source D and use your own knowledge. Why was the photograph taken? Use details from the photograph and your own knowledge to explain the answer. (Remember how to answer this type of question? For further guidance, see page 23.)*

5. *What can you learn from Source C about Nixon's attitude to the student movement? (Remember how to answer this type of question? For further guidance, see page 16.)*

6. *Study Sources E, F and G. How far do these sources agree about the events at Kent State University? (Remember how to answer this type of question? For further guidance, see pages 60–61.)*

7. *Put together a headline in a US national newspaper the day after the Kent State University deaths.*

The 'hippy' movement

Other young people protested in a totally different way. They decided to 'drop out' of society and become hippies. This meant they grew their hair long, wore distinctive clothes and developed an 'alternative lifestyle'. Often they travelled round the country in buses and vans, and wore flowers in their hair as a symbol of peace rather than war. Indeed, their slogan was 'make love, not war'.

Because they often wore flowers and handed them out to police, they were called 'flower children', and they often settled in communes. San Francisco became the hippy capital of America. Their behaviour, especially their use of drugs, frequently led to clashes with the police, who they nicknamed 'pigs'.

They were influenced by groups such as the Grateful Dead and the Doors. The highlight of the movement came at the Woodstock and Altamont rock concerts at the end of the 1960s (see Source H).

This movement was of particular concern to the older generation because:

- They refused to work.
- They experimented with drugs such as marijuana and LSD.
- Many were from middle-class and not under-privileged backgrounds. They rejected all the values that their parents believed in.

Student radicalism

In the later 1960s, the student movement became more radical in its views. Some of its members called themselves 'Weathermen' and began to support violence to achieve their aims. They took their name from the Bob Dylan song 'You Don't Need a Weatherman to Know Which Way the Wind Blows'. They bombed army recruitment centres and government buildings. Tom Hayden disapproved of this extremism and left the movement in 1970.

Source H: A group of hippies wearing typical 'hippy' clothes, drumming together before the start of the Woodstock festival in 1969

Source I: Jim Morrison, lead singer of the group the Doors, 1969

I like ideas about the breaking away or overthrowing of established order. I am interested in anything about revolt, disorder, chaos, especially activity that seems to have no meaning. It seems to me to be the road towards freedom – external freedom is a way to bring about internal freedom.

Tasks

8. *What can you learn from Source H about the hippy movement? (Remember how to answer this type of question? For further guidance, see page 16.)*

9. *Study Source I. Why do you think Jim Morrison made this statement?*

10. *Have you ever played the game Pictionary?*
- *You have to explain the meaning of a word to someone else using an illustration.*
- *They have to guess the word you are illustrating.*
Try this out on a friend or relative with the word 'hippy' and one other new word from this section on student protest.

Why was the student movement important?

What influence did the student movement have on the issues for which it campaigned, such as civil rights, greater freedom and the war in Vietnam?

Youth culture

In many respects, the longest-lasting achievement was on youth culture itself. By the end of the 1960s, there were profound changes in the whole lifestyle of the young. This was partly reflected in fashion, with the young becoming far more fashion-conscious and determined to move away from the 'norm' of the older generation. This is best shown by the miniskirt, which was also a reflection of the greater **sexual permissiveness**. Teenagers became much more aware of their individuality and demanded a greater say in what they wore and did.

Vietnam

Although the SDS and student protest did not bring an end to the war in Vietnam, there is no doubt that they helped to force a shift in government policy and make the withdrawal from Vietnam much more likely. They certainly influenced President Johnson's decision not to seek re-election in 1968.

Racism

In addition, they provided greater publicity for the racism still prevalent in US society. The support of many white students for black civil rights strengthened the whole movement and showed that most American youths would no longer tolerate **discrimination** and **segregation**.

Middle-class origins

Finally, it should be remembered that the bulk of the students were of middle-class origin. They would have been expected to support the government in most areas. For such people to oppose the government on key issues (and in some cases oppose their families' views) was virtually unheard of, and shook the older, more conservative generation.

Source A: A photograph taken at an anti-Vietnam War demonstration in 1968

Tasks

1. *Study Source A and use your own knowledge. Why was this photograph taken? Use details from the source and your own knowledge to explain the answer. (Remember how to answer this type of question? For further guidance, see page 23.)*

2. *Describe the key features of the student movement.*

3. *Youth culture underwent great changes in the 1960s. Fashion is one example. Research one more example and prepare a one-minute talk on its key changes. Here are some possible areas of research:*
   - *US television for the young*
   - *the film industry*
   - *new dance crazes*
   - *magazines and advertisements*
   - *changes in male youth's fashion*
   - *other protest singers.*

Examination practice

This section provides guidance on how to answer the hypothesis testing question from Unit 3, which is worth sixteen marks.

In this question you are asked to explain an interpretation using:
- five or six sources
- your own knowledge

At each level, you should make judgments on the reliability and sufficiency of the sources. Sufficiency means how much do the sources explain or show about the event or person.

The examiner would expect you to write between one and two sides of A4. Here is a mark scheme for the hypothesis testing question:

Level	Descriptor	Marks
2	A supported answer that supports or disagrees with the interpretation and comments on the reliability of the sources.	5–8
3	A developed answer that supports and disagrees with the interpretation using the sources and your own knowledge, although the answer may lack balance. Comments on the reliability or sufficiency of the sources.	9–12
4	A fully balanced answer which uses precisely selected material from the sources and own knowledge. The reliability and sufficiency of sources taken into account in coming to a conclusion.	13–16

Question 1 – hypothesis testing

'The hippy movement was the main reason for increased support for the student movement in the years to 1970.'

How far do Sources A–F support this statement? Use details from the sources and your own knowledge to explain your answer.

Source A: From *The Hippie Generation* by Adam Huber, Chris Lemieux and Marlon Hollis, 2004

During the 1960s a radical group called the hippies shocked America with their alternative lifestyle and radical beliefs. They were young people who enjoyed life to its fullest. They used illegal drugs and listened to rock and roll music. With their alternative beliefs and practices they stunned America's conservative middle class. Concerned chiefly with protesting against the Vietnam War and with civil rights, they made a huge impact on America and the world and attracted many young people to the student protest movement.

Source B: From a history of the USA 1917–80, written in 1996

During the second half of the 1960s many young people turned against the lifestyles of their parents. Their behaviour challenged the established values of older people. Hippy clothes, with long hair and mystical religion, became fashionable, along with the use of drugs and permissive sexual behaviour. 'Make love not war' was their slogan.

Source C: Julian Bond, a leading member of the black civil rights movement in the 1960s, interviewed in 2003

Both the war in Vietnam and black civil rights encouraged greater support for the student movement. In 1966, both the Student Nonviolent Coordinating Committee and the Black Panther Party adopted strong antiwar positions. That was also the year that the heavyweight boxing champion of the world, Muhammad Ali, refused induction to the military and was stripped of his boxing title.

Source D: A student slogan against the war in Vietnam

Hey! Hey! LBJ [Lyndon B Johnson]
How many kids did you kill today?
We don't want your war
Draft beer, not boys
Dump Johnson
Eighteen Today, Dead Tomorrow

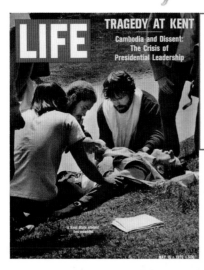

Source E: The cover of *Life*, showing one of the students killed at Kent State University, May 1970

Source F: From a speech by Martin Luther King in 1967

We were taking the young black men who had been ruined by our society and sending them 8,000 miles away to defend freedom in South East Asia – a freedom which they have not found in their own country. Instead we have repeatedly seen the cruel image of the negro and white boys on TV screens as they kill and die together in a nation that has been unable to provide schools in which negro and white children can sit together.

How to answer

Make a copy of the grid below and use it to help you plan your answer. Advice on how to write your answer is given on page 100.

1. First study Sources A–F.
- Which sources agree with the interpretation? Why? Give a brief explanation in the grid. An example is given below.
- Which sources disagree with the interpretation? Why? Give a brief explanation in the grid. An example has been done for you.

2. Now briefly make a judgement on the reliability of each source. For further guidance refer to page 89.
- In what ways is each source reliable? An example has been done for you.
- In what ways is each source unreliable? An example has been done for you.

3. Now use your own contextual knowledge of the student movement to back up:
- the source(s) which agree with the interpretation. Summarise this in your grid.
- the source(s) which disagree with the interpretation. Summarise this in the grid. An example has been done for you.

	Agrees with interpretation	Disagrees with interpretation	Reliable	Unreliable
Source A				
Source B	Suggests that many young people turned to hippy lifestyle.			
Source C				
Source D			Reflects the views of many students against the president, due to many deaths in the war.	Exaggerates and simplifies the role of Johnson in order to turn people against the president and the war.
Source E		Suggests it was opposition to the war.		
Source F				Speech in which King may exaggerate in order to win support.

	Agrees with interpretation	Disagrees with interpretation
Own knowledge		Source D suggests that the war in Vietnam was the main reason. This is supported by the knowledge that many students feared being called up.

The diagram below gives you the steps you should take to write a good hypothesis testing answer. Use the steps and examples to complete the answer to the question on page 98.

STEP 1
Write an introduction that identifies the key issues you need to cover in your answer and your main argument.

Example:
The student movement originated in the early 1960s and became associated with the hippy movement. It was encouraged, as some of the sources suggest, by the 'drop-out' lifestyle of the hippies as well as popular music of the time. However, as other sources suggest, the conflict in Vietnam proved one of the main reasons for its growth, especially in the second half of the 1960s.

STEP 2
After your introduction, write a good length paragraph or paragraphs agreeing with the interpretation. Begin each paragraph with a sentence that focuses on the question, followed by your own knowledge and using any of the sources which agree with the interpretation.

Example:
Sources A and B suggest that the hippy movement was the main reason for increased support for the student movement in the 1960s. Source A suggests that the hippy movement attracted many young people to the student movement and played an important role in the civil rights movement and the campaign against the war in Vietnam.

STEP 3
Have a go yourself using any other sources that agree with the interpretation, reinforced by your own contextual knowledge.

STEP 4
Make judgements on the reliability of the sources that agree with the interpretation.

Example:
Source A does provide evidence of the importance of the hippy movement. However, it is unreliable as it is possibly written by supporters of the hippy movement, who may be exaggerating its importance in the 1960s.

STEP 5
Have a go yourself at evaluating the reliability of any other sources you have used in this section.

Example:
However, sources C, D, E and F suggest that the most important reason for increased support for the student movement was the conflict in Vietnam. Source D provides evidence of the opposition to the war and suggests that many students blamed President Johnson for the draft system and for the increased number of deaths after 1966.

STEP 6
Write a good length paragraph or paragraphs disagreeing with the interpretation. Begin each paragraph with a sentence that focuses on the question, followed by your own knowledge and using any of the sources which disagree with the interpretation.

STEP 7
Have a go yourself using any other sources that disagree with the interpretation and any other own knowledge.

STEP 8
Make judgements on the reliability of the sources which disagree with the interpretation.

Example:
Source D provides reliable evidence of a popular student protest song and their strong feelings against the president. However, it does exaggerate the role of Johnson in order to win support for the anti-war movement.

STEP 9
Have a go yourself at evaluating the reliability of any other sources you have used in this section.

Example:
For the most part I disagree with the interpretation. Although Sources A and B suggest that the hippy movement was popular, it was very much a movement for peace and an offshoot of the events in Vietnam. Sources C, D, E and F suggest that the student movement won much support from those who not only opposed US involvement in the conflict, but also feared being drafted into the armed forces.

STEP 10
Write a conclusion giving your final judgement on the interpretation. Do you mainly agree or disagree? Explain your judgement.

The women's movement

Source A: A table produced by the US Department of Labour. It shows the average wages of men and women in 1965.

	Men	Women
Factory workers	$5,752	$3,282
Service industries	$4,886	$2,784
Sales staff	$7,083	$3,003
Clerical	$6,220	$4,237
Professional	$8,233	$5,573
Managers, executives	$8,658	$4,516

Task

What can you learn from Source A about the reasons for the women's movement? (Remember how to answer this type of question? For further guidance, see page 16.)

The women's movement was launched in 1963 by a very influential book, *The Feminine Mystique*, by Betty Friedan. Three years later Friedan and others sets up the National Organization for women (NOW). Supporters of the movement used petitions, strikes and legal action to improve the employment opportunities and pay of women. More extreme campaigners, known as the Women's Liberation Movement, campaigned against male sexism – including the Miss America Pageant – and were often ridiculed by men. Some women, led by Phyllis Schlafly, actively opposed the women's movement and the attempt to achieve equal rights.

This chapter answers the following questions:

- What was the impact of the Second World War?
- How did the women's movement emerge?
- What did the women's movement achieve?
- How did the women's movement develop?
- What links were there between the protest movements?

Examination skills

In this chapter you will be given the opportunity to answer some of the question types from Unit 3.

What was the impact of the Second World War?

Before 1941, American women had a traditional role as wives and mothers, and few of them had careers. There were few real opportunities except in typically 'female' professions such as teaching, nursing and secretarial work.

Socially, however, the 1920s had seen much progress, especially in urban areas. Some women wore more daring clothes, smoked and drank with men in public. They went out with men, in cars, without a chaperone – and even kissed in public. In addition, in 1921 women over twenty were given the vote. The Second World War had mixed results for the position of women.

Progress

Women made a great contribution to the war effort and this opened up many new areas of employment for working-class women, especially in producing munitions. Indeed, the pay in 'munitions' work was much higher than that normally paid to women in 'female' occupations. The number of women in employment increased from twelve million in 1940 to 18.5 million five years later. Many of these new jobs were in traditionally 'male' occupations such as the shipyards, aircraft factories and munitions. Women proved that they could do these jobs and, in 1942, a poll showed that 60 per cent of Americans were in favour of women helping with the war industries.

Women also joined the armed forces, with about 300,000 serving in the women's sections of the army, navy and the nursing corps.

So, in certain respects the position of women improved. They had shown they could do jobs that traditionally had been male-dominated. Four US states made equal pay for women compulsory, while other states tried to protect women from discrimination in their jobs. In 1940, women made up nineteen per cent of the workforce. This had risen to 28.8 per cent ten years later.

Lack of progress

Nevertheless, at the end of the war:

- The majority of women willingly gave up their wartime jobs and returned to their role as mothers and wives and their traditional 'female' jobs.
- Women were generally excluded from the top, well-paid jobs.
- Women, on average, earned 50–60 per cent of the wage that men earned for doing the same job.
- Women could still be dismissed from their job when they married.

Source A: **A poster from wartime USA featuring Rosie the Riveter, 1942. Rosie the Riveter was a fictional female worker used by the US government in a poster campaign to encourage women to help with the war effort. There was even a movie made about her.**

Source B: US service women, who were in a contest to find the most attractive woman in the US armed forces, 1944

Source C: Peggy Terry describing her work in a munitions factory in Kentucky during the Second World War

I pulled a lot of gadgets on a machine. Tetryl was one of the ingredients we used and it turned us orange. Our hands, our face, our neck just turned orange, even our eyeballs. We never questioned … The only thing we worried about was other women thinking we had dyed our hair. Back then it was a disgrace if you dyed your hair. I remember a woman on a bus saying that she hoped the war would not end until she got her refrigerator paid for.

Tasks

1. *What can you learn from Source C about the role of women during the Second World War? (Remember how to answer this type of question? For further guidance, see page 16.)*

2. *Study Source A and use your own knowledge. What was the purpose of the poster? Use details from the poster and your own knowledge to explain the answer. (Remember how to answer this type of question? For further guidance, see page 34.)*

3. *Copy and fill in the following table by studying sources A, B and C. For each source decide whether it shows progress in the position of women or a lack of progress. Give a brief explanation for your choice. You may feel that one or more of the sources show both.*

Source	Progress	Lack of progress
A		
B		
C		

How did the women's movement emerge?

What was the position of women, 1945–60?

The Second World War had seen some progress in the position of women but, for the most part, this did not continue for the generation of women that followed. Indeed, there was much media influence encouraging women to adopt their traditional family role (see Sources A, B and C).

Women who went out to work instead of getting married were treated with great suspicion by the rest of society. Indeed, one very influential book, *Modern Women: the Lost Sex*, actually blamed many of the social problems of the 1950s, such as teenage drinking and delinquency, on career women.

Source A: The typical 'mother' image from the 1950s

Source B: From *The Woman's Guide to Better Living*, written in the 1950s

Whether you are a man or woman, the family is the unit to which you most genuinely belong. The family is the centre of your living. If it isn't, you've gone astray.

Source C: From the 1955 film *The Tender Trap* – a conversation between two of the leading characters in the film, Debbie Reynolds and Frank Sinatra

Reynolds: The theatre's all right, but its only temporary.
Sinatra: Are you thinking of something else?
Reynolds: Marriage, I hope. A career is just fine, but it's no substitute for marriage. Don't you think a man is just the most important thing in the world? A woman isn't a woman until she's been married and had children.

Task

1. *How far do Sources A, B and C support the view that the women's role was in the home?*
(Remember how to answer this type of question? For further guidance, see pages 60–61)

The 1950s

In the 1950s, growing numbers of women, especially from middle-class backgrounds, began to challenge their traditional role, as they became increasingly frustrated with life as a housewife. There was more to life than bringing up children and looking after their husbands. Women were now much better educated, so they could have a professional career. In 1950, there were 721,000 women at university. By 1960, this had reached 1.3 million. However, many of these women had a very limited choice of career because, once they married, they were expected to devote their energies to their husband and children. Many became increasingly bored and frustrated with life as a suburban housewife.

Despite post-war attitudes, the number of women in employment continued to increase – they were seen by many employers as a valuable source of cheap, often part-time labour. In 1950, women made up 29 per cent of the workforce. By 1960, this was almost 50 per cent.

The 1960s

Many female teenagers were strongly influenced by the greater freedom of the 'Swinging Sixties' (see page 86) which, in turn, encouraged them to challenge traditional attitudes and roles. Moreover, the contraceptive pill gave females much greater choice about when or whether to have children. This could be prevented or postponed whilst a woman pursued her career.

Eleanor Roosevelt, the widow of President Roosevelt, made an important contribution to the cause when, in 1960, she set up a commission to investigate the status of women at work. Eleanor had been a keen supporter of women's rights since the 1920s and, during her husband Franklin D. Roosevelt's presidency (1933–45), she had actively campaigned for full equality for women in American political life. President Kennedy appointed Eleanor Roosevelt to chair the commission, but she died just before it issued its final report.

The results were reported in 1963 and highlighted women's second-class status in employment. For example, 95 per cent of company managers were men and 85 per cent of technical workers. Only seven per cent of doctors were women and even less – four per cent – were lawyers. Women only earned 50 to 60 per cent of the wages of men who did the same job and generally had low-paid jobs.

Another woman, Betty Friedan, was even more influential in the emergence of the woman's movement. In 1963 she wrote *The Feminine Mystique*. Her book expressed the thoughts of many women – there was more to life than being a mother and housewife. Indeed the expression 'The Feminine Mystique' was her term for the idea that a woman's happiness was all tied up with her domestic role (see Source D).

Friedan was important because she called for women to reject this 'mystique' and demanded progress in female employment opportunities. She insisted that bringing up a family should be a shared role, which would enable the wife to pursue a career if she wanted. Disillusioned with the lack of progress in employment opportunities despite government legislation in 1963 and 1964, in 1966 she set up the National Organization for Women (NOW).

Source D: From *The Feminine Mystique*, by Betty Friedan, 1963

The problem lay buried, unspoken for many years in the minds of American women. It was a strange stirring, a sense of dissatisfaction, a yearning that women suffered in the middle of the twentieth century in the United States.

Tasks

2. *How useful is Source D as evidence of the position of women in the USA in the early 1960s?*

3. *Write letters to a local newspaper from two US women who have read Betty Friedan's* The Feminine Mystique *in the mid-1960s:*
- *one giving reasons in support of Friedan's views*
- *one opposing them and giving the traditional view of women.*

What did the women's movement achieve?

Date	Key development	Achievement	Limitation
1963	Equal Pay Act	Required employers to pay women the same as men for the same job.	It did not address the issue of discrimination against women seeking jobs in the first place.
1964	Civil Rights Act	Made it illegal to discriminate on the grounds of gender.	The Equal Opportunities Commission did not take female discrimination seriously, so the Act was not fully enforced.
1966	National Organization for Women (NOW)	This was set up by mainly white middle-class women in order to attack obvious examples of discrimination. By the early 1940s, it had 40,000 members and had organised demonstrations in American cities. They challenged discrimination in the courts and in a series of cases between 1966 and 1971, secured $30 million in back pay owed to women who had not been paid wages equal to men.	Methods were too moderate and progress too slow for more extreme campaigners. It was often very difficult to prove discrimination in employment through the law courts.
1967	Sport	Women were not allowed to compete in marathons but in 1967 a sole woman entered the Boston Marathon, having registered for it without giving her name. Two years later came the first national athletics championships for women students.	Billie Jean King won many tennis tournaments in the later 1960s, including Wimbledon three times. However, she was paid far less than male winners. For example, in 1970 she received $600 for winning the Italian Championships, while the men's winner pocketed $3,500.
1970	Equal Rights Amendment	In February, about 20 NOW members, led by Wilma Scott Heide and Jean Witter, disrupted the **Senate** hearings on the eighteen-year-old vote to demand hearings on the Equal Rights Amendment Act. At a signal from Heide, the women rose and unfolded posters they had concealed in their purses.	The Educational Rights Act became bogged down in **Congress** and was finally defeated by three votes in 1982.

Table showing achievements and limitations of the women's movement in the 1960s.

Source A: The NOW Bill of Rights, which was agreed at NOW's first national conference of 1967

1. Equal Rights Constitution Amendment
2. Enforce Law Banning Sex
3. Maternity Leave Rights in Employment and Social Security Benefits
4. Tax Deduction for Home and Child Care Expenses for Working Parents
5. Child Day Care Centres
6. Equal and Unsegregated Education
7. Equal Job Training Opportunities and Allowances for Women to Control Their Reproductive Lives.

Tasks

1. *What can you learn from Source A about the aims of NOW? (Remember how to answer this type of question? For further guidance, see page 16)*

2. *Study Source B. Have the employment opportunities for women improved in the years 1950–80?*

3. *Make a copy of the scales and list the achievements and limitations of the women's movement. Overall, was it a success? Explain your answer.*

Achievements   Limitations

Source B: The percentage of women working in various occupations in the years 1950–70

Occupational group	1950	1960	1970
All workers	28	33	38
White-collar	40	43	48
Professional	40	38	40
Managerial	14	14	17
Clerical	62	68	74
Sales	34	37	39
Blue-collar	24	26	30
Crafts	3	3	5
Operatives	27	28	32
Labourers	4	4	8
Private households	95	96	96
Other services	45	52	55
Farm workers	9	10	10

How did the women's movement develop?

The Women's Liberation Movement

The Women's Liberation Movement was the name given to women who had far more radical aims than NOW. They were also known as **feminists** and were much more active in challenging discrimination. Indeed, the really extreme feminists wanted nothing to do with men. All signs of male supremacy were to be removed, including male control of employment, politics and the media.

They believed that even not wearing make-up was an act of protest against male supremacy and were determined to get as much publicity for their cause as possible. For example, they burned their bras, as these were also seen as a symbol of male domination. In 1968, others picketed the Miss America beauty contest in Atlantic City (see Source A) and even crowned a sheep 'Miss America'. The whole contest, they argued, degraded the position of women. However, the activities of the Women's Liberation Movement did more harm than good. Their extreme actions and protests brought the wrong sort of publicity. Burning their bras in public brought ridicule to the movement and made it increasingly difficult for men and other women to take the whole issue of women's rights seriously. They were a distraction from the key issues of equal pay and better job opportunities.

Source B: A photograph from a national newspaper showing a demonstration by members of the Women's Liberation Group in August 1970

Source A: Members of the Women's Liberation Movement hold protest signs outside the Miss America Pageant (contest), in Atlantic City, 7 September 1968

Tasks

1. Study Source A.
- Devise a catchy newspaper headline for a local Atlantic City newspaper describing this scene.
- Write an editorial giving the newspaper's views of this event and the Women's Liberation Movement. Bear in mind that newspaper proprietors and editors would probably have been male.

2. How useful is Source B as evidence of the activities of the women's liberation movement?

The campaign to legalise abortion

Abortion was illegal in the USA. Feminists challenged this, arguing it was wrong to force women to have a child they did not want, and began to challenge this through courts of law. The struggle against abortion began in the early 1960s when a young medical technician, Estelle Griswold, challenged the anti-abortion laws in her home state of Connecticut, where abortion and contraceptive devices – and even giving information about contraception – were illegal.

Her lawyers acted very astutely by not directly challenging the abortion laws. Their argument was that these laws were an illegal restriction on the privacy of ordinary Americans, which was part of the Fourteenth Amendment of the US constitution. The case went to the **Supreme Court**, which ruled 7–2 in favour of Griswold in 1965.

This case encouraged later challenges to abortion, most notably the Roe v. Wade case that began in 1970. A feminist lawyer, Sarah Weddington, defended the right of one of her clients, Norma McCorvey, named Jane Roe to protect her anonymity, to have an abortion. She already had three children, who had all been taken into care, and did not want any more children. She won the right to have an abortion. The victory led to abortions becoming more readily available.

Opposition to the women's movement

Some women opposed the women's movement:

- Some because they believed that NOW was dominated by white, middle-class females.
- Others objected to the extreme demands and methods of the Women's Liberation Movement.
- A number genuinely believed in and accepted the traditional role of women.
- Some women were anti-abortion.
- The women's movement did not seem to be doing enough to help poor women.

One of the most influential opponents was Phyllis Schlafly, who set up STOP ERA. Schlafly was an author and had been active in politics, standing for Congress on several occasions between 1952 and 1970. ERA stood for the Equal Rights Amendment, proposed by NOW in 1967, to change the US constitution to guarantee women equality. Schlafly organised a highly successful campaign to stop ERA

Source C: Quotes made by Phyllis Schlafly

'What I am defending is the real rights of women. A woman should have the right to be in the home as a wife and mother.'

'Feminism is doomed to failure because it is based on an attempt to repeal and restructure human nature.'

'Sexual harassment on the job is not a problem for virtuous women.'

'Men should stop treating feminists like ladies, and instead treat them like the men they say they want to be.'

and ensured that this amendment to the constitution was delayed until 1982, when it was finally defeated by three votes. She opposed ERA because it would require women to serve in combat and thought it would have a bad influence on family life.

Tasks

3. What can you learn from Source C about Phyllis Schlafly's views of the women's movement? (Remember how to answer this type of question? For further guidance, see page 16.)

4. Put together two concept maps:
- one showing the achievements of the women's movement
- the other showing its limitations.

Here are some facts and figures to help you.
- In 1970, 44 per cent of men earned over $25,000 a year, while only nine per cent of women did.
- The percentage of women in professional and managerial positions remained much the same in the years 1950–70.
- By 1970 other women's groups had been set up, such as the National Women's Caucus and the Women's Campaign Fund.
- By 1970, 40 per cent of university students were female.
- 80 per cent of teachers were women but only 10 per cent of principals (head teachers).
- 7 per cent of doctors and 3 per cent of lawyers were female by the end of the 1960s.
- In November 1968, NOW member Shirley Chisholm became the first black woman elected to the US House of Representatives.

What links were there between the protest movements?

The 1960s and 1970s saw a variety of protest movements in the USA on issues as diverse as black and female civil rights, the war in Vietnam and student education. However, as you have seen, these protest groups generally did not act in isolation. One often led to or supported the other. For example, Martin Luther King's peaceful methods provided the inspiration for other protest groups.

Tasks

1. *Below are four pictures, each showing the main protest movements.*
- *On a piece of A3 size paper draw four boxes to represent the pictures below, and label each with the title of the movement, as below.*
- *Draw different coloured lines from one box to another to show the links between two or more of these protest movements.*
- *On your line explain the link.*
One example has been done for you.

2. *What is an acrostic? See if you can do one for the word 'protest':*

P
R
O
T
E
S
T

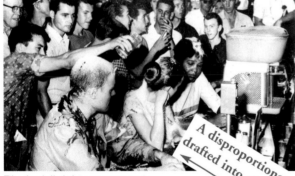

Black civil rights movement

Women's movement

Student movement

A disproportionate number of black youths were drafted into the armed forces and sent to Vietnam

Anti-Vietnam War movement

Examination practice

On the next two pages you will be given the opportunity to practise all five of the question types in Unit 3. The questions about the sources are on page 112.

Source A: From a history of the USA, 1917–80, written in 1996

Feminists used petitions, strikes and legal action to push employers to increase wages and open top-level jobs to women. At the same time, women were encouraged to protest against male sexism. Women invaded all-male bars and clubs, burned men's magazines that they said exploited women and urged married women to keep their own surnames.

Source C: From the original declaration of the National Organization of Women, 1966

We believe the time has come to move beyond the argument, and discussion over the status and special nature of women which has raged in America in recent years. The time has come to confront, with concrete action, the conditions that now prevent women from enjoying the equality of opportunity and freedom of choice which is their right, as individual Americans, and as human beings.

Source B: A photograph of 1968 in a national newspaper, showing a secretary in San Francisco about to burn her bra in support of the women's liberation movement

Source D: From *The Feminine Mystique*, by Betty Friedan, 1963

Each suburban wife struggled with it alone. As she made the beds, shopped for groceries, matched slipcover material, ate peanut butter sandwiches with her children, chauffered Cub Scouts and Brownies, lay beside her husband at night — she was afraid to ask even of herself the silent question – 'Is this all?'

Source F: From a modern world history, published in 1997

There were also women who wanted nothing to do with the issue of women's rights at all. They objected to feminist slogans which described men as the enemy. One group, led by Phyllis Schlafly, opposed the Equal Rights Amendment Act (ERA) which would guarantee women equality as part of the constitution. Schlafly set up the STOP ERA movement. The opponents won and ERA narrowly failed to become part of the constitution because only 35 of the 38 states needed voted to support it.

Question 1 – inference
Study Source A.
What can you learn from Source A about the methods used by the Women's Liberation Movement? (6 marks)
(Remember how to answer this type of question? For further guidance, see page 16.)

Question 2 – source interpretation
Study Source B and use your own knowledge.
Why was this photograph so widely publicised? Use details from the photograph and your own knowledge to explain the answer. (8 marks)
(Remember how to answer this type of question? For further guidance, see page 23.)

Question 3 – cross-referencing
Study Sources A, B and C and use your own knowledge.
How far do these sources agree about the activities of the women's movement in the USA in the 1960s? Explain your answer. (10 marks)
(Remember how to answer this type of question? For further guidance, see page 60–61.)

Question 4 – utility
Study Sources D and E.
How useful are Sources D and E as evidence of the importance of Betty Friedan? Explain your answer using the sources and your own knowledge. (10 marks)
(Remember how to answer this type of question? For further guidance, see pages 72–73.)

Question 5 – hypothesis testing
Study all the sources and use your own knowledge.
'The women's movement was successful in the USA in the 1960s.'
How far do Sources A–F (pages 111–12) support this statement? Use details from the sources and your own knowledge to explain your answer. (16 marks)
(Remember how to answer this type of question? For further guidance, see pages 98–100.)

Revision activities

Key Topic 1: McCarthyism and the Red Scare

1. Place the following events in the Cold War in chronological order:

- China becomes communist
- Korean War
- Churchill and the 'Iron Curtain' speech
- Potsdam Conference
- Berlin airlift
- Marshall Plan
- Setting up NATO
- Truman Doctrine

2. Insert the following missing words from the passage about the Cold War.

> Greece • hostility • Iron Curtain • East
> • worsened • Marshall • Doctrine

The war ended in August 1945, and throughout the first months of peace, relations between the two Superpowers .... and Truman was advised to 'contain Russian expansive tendencies'. In March 1946, Churchill talked of an .... separating the West and the .... in Europe – there seemed to be clear .... between the former allies. Events in Europe continued to widen the gap – the British inability to stem communism in .... led President Truman to issue the Truman ...., and the supreme effort to contain communism came with the .... Plan.

3. What do the following initials stand for?

- HUAC
- FBI
- FELP

4. Categorise the importance of the following reasons for the build-up of the Red Scare in the USA, beginning with the most important to the least important.

- Hoover and FBI
- HUAC
- Rosenbergs
- Hiss case

5. True or false?

	True	False
McCarthy was a Republican senator		
Kennedy was president during the McCarthy era		
McCarthy stated that he had 405 names in his suitcase		
McCarthy was made Chairman of the Government Committee on Operations of the Senate		
Ed Murrow was the attorney for the army		
Joseph Welsh was the TV presenter who exposed McCarthy		
McCarthy died in 1957		

6. Explain, in no more than a sentence, what you know about the following in connection with McCarthyism and the Red Scare:

- Ed Murrow
- Joseph Welsh
- Richard Nixon
- The McCarran Act
- The Hollywood Ten

1. Explain in no more than two sentences what you know about the following:

- segregation
- discrimination
- Executive Order 8802
- CORE
- NAACP
- Dixiecrats

2. Choose one of the following interpretations about the US education system in the 1950s and write a paragraph justifying the statement.

- There was considerable change in the US education system in the 1950s.
- There was some change in the US education system in the 1950s.
- There was little change in the US education system in the 1950s.

3. Which of the statements best sums up the success of the Montgomery Bus Boycott? Give reasons for your decision.

- It succeeded because of the car-pooling.
- It succeeded because of Martin Luther King.
- The Supreme Court intervened.

4. Make a copy of the following table and decide the importance of each of the following events in the Montgomery Bus Boycott. Explain your choice.

5. Summarise in no more than TWENTY words the importance of the following in the civil rights campaigns.

Direct action	
Sit-ins	
Civil Rights Act, 1957	
SNCC	

6. 'The freedom rides were a complete success.' Write TWO paragraphs disagreeing with this statement.

	Of little importance	Quite important	Important	Very important
Rosa Parks				
Jo Ann Robinson				
Montgomery Improvement Association (MIA)				

1. The following account about events in Birmingham is by a student who has not revised thoroughly. Rewrite the account, correcting any errors.

King decided to March to Birmingham in 1964 and in August the demonstrations began. King was arrested and he wrote his famous 'Article from Birmingham Prison'. On his release, President Kennedy sent troops and an agreement was reached to end segregation in Birmingham. At the end of the trouble Evers Medgar, a leader of CORE, was shot.

2. What explanation can you give for the following statements?

• The March on Washington was a success.
• Malcolm X was correct when he called the march the 'farce on Washington'.

3. Place the following events in chronological order:

• Voting Rights Act
• 'Freedom Summer'
• Civil Rights Act
• Assassination of President Kennedy
• Assassination of Martin Luther King
• Murder of civil rights activists Chaney, Goodman and Schwerner
• Selma marches

4. Explain in no more than one sentence what you know about the following:

• Bloody Sunday 1965
• 'Great Society'
• New Frontier
• Literacy tests

5. Make a copy of the table and summarise in no more than TWENTY words the importance of each in the civil rights movement in the 1960s.

Malcolm X	
Black Power	
Black Panthers	
The death of Martin Luther King	

6. 'The civil rights campaigns had been a complete success by 1970.' Write TWO paragraphs disagreeing with this statement.

1. Pair the following sentences together.

(a) One of the most influential singer/songwriters of the 1960s was Bob Dylan.
(b) The assassination of JFK also encouraged support for the student movement.
(c) The student movement was also encouraged by worldwide events.

(i) He had tried to harness the youth of America to his reform programme and captured the support of many.
(ii) For example, in the late 1960s there were student protests in Northern Ireland and in Paris.
(iii) He was important because many of his songs attacked the injustice and intolerance of US society.

2. The following account of the reasons for the student movement is by a student who has not revised thoroughly. Rewrite the account, correcting any errors.

Much support for the student movement was because of US involvement in the conflict in Korea. As the number of US casualties fell, so the number of supporters increased. Many students were afraid of the draft system which gave them the choice of whether or not to join up. One of the most famous protests took place at Kent State University, Chicago, in 1970, when six people were killed.

3. What were the following?
(a) The SDS
(b) The hippy movement
(c) Woodstock
(d) The Weathermen

4. Insert the following missing words from the passage about the student movement.

segregation • youth culture • Vietnam • 1968
• Johnson's • lifestyle • white • racism

In many respects, the most long-lasting achievement was in ………… By the end of the 1960s there were profound changes in the ………….. of the young. Although the SDS did not bring an end to the war in ………………., there is no doubt that they influenced President …………… decision not to seek re-election in ……….. In addition, they gave greater publicity to …………. in US society. Many ………… students supported black students in the campaign against discrimination and ……………

5. Place the following events in the women's movement in chronological order
• Roe v. Wade case
• Eleanor Roosevelt Commission
• Miss America Beauty Pageant in Atlantic City
• *Feminine Mystique*
• Civil Rights Act
• Setting up of NOW

6. Place the following statements about the protest movements of the 1960s in the correct circle. If you believe it involved both the student and women's movement then place it in the overlapping circle.

• Inspired by protest singers
• Supported civil rights for black Americans
• Influenced by the 'Swinging Sixties'
• Campaigned against the war in Vietnam
• Demanded a greater say in university education
• Wanted greater employment opportunities
• Picketed the Miss America Beauty Pageant
• Some became members of the 'hippy' movement
• NOW was the main organisation
• SDS was the main group

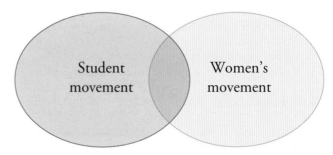

Glossary

Armistice An agreement for a temporary end to hostilities.

Attorney General Chief legal officer of the US government.

Battle of the Bulge Hitler's last assault on allied forces in the West.

Bolshevik Revolution Communist takeover in Russia in October 1917.

Bolsheviks The political group led by Lenin. They believed in communism.

Capitalism Private ownership of industry and agriculture.

CIA Central Investigation Agency, the secret service responsible for security inside and outside the USA. Organises spying.

Civil rights The campaign for equal social, economic and political rights and opportunities.

Cominform Communist Information Bureau set up by Stalin in 1947 to ensure greater control of the communist parties in the countries of Eastern Europe.

Communism Political theory that put forward the idea of state ownership of industry and agriculture.

Communist A believer in the theory that society should be classless, private property abolished, and land and businesses owned collectively. Following the Communist Revolution in Russia in 1917, there had been a growing fear that communism might spread to the USA and destroy the system of government.

Congress The US equivalent of parliament is Congress. Congress is split into two parts, the Senate and the House of Representatives.

Congress of Racial Equality (CORE) Established in 1942 by James Farmer. CORE was the first organisation in the USA to use the tactic of sit-ins.

Conscription Where males of a certain age (usually 18–41) have to serve in the armed forces for a period of time.

Democrat Someone belonging to the Democratic Party, one of the two parties in the USA, which tended to follow policies of government intervention and favoured measures to improve health, welfare and education.

Desegregation Removal of the policy of separation.

Direct action Ways of making demands known through sit-ins, sit-down demonstrations and boycotts.

Discrimination Unfair treatment of individuals because of their gender, race or religious beliefs.

Disenfranchisement Taking away the right to vote.

Dixiecrats Democrat Party senators from the southern states.

Draft US method of recruitment into the armed forces. It was compulsory for men (youths) who reached the age of eighteen to serve in the armed forces.

Enfranchise To give an individual the right to vote.

FBI Federal Bureau of Investigation, set up to investigate organised crime.

Federal government The central government of the USA, which is based in Washington, DC.

Feminist Supporter of women's rights who believes that men and women are equal in all areas.

Fifth Amendment Part of the US constitution that allows the accused person in a trial not to be forced to give testimony.

Ghetto A densely populated area of a city inhabited by a socially and economically deprived minority.

Inauguration speech The speech given by a president at his swearing-in ceremony (inauguration).

Iron curtain Term used by Winston Churchill to describe the imaginary barrier between East and West Europe.

Ku Klux Klan A secret society of white people in the American south who believed in white supremacy and resorted to violence against black people as well as Jews and other minority groups.

Lynching When a mob kills someone for a cause they believe in, without the due process of law.

Marshall Plan Introduced by the USA in 1947 to provide aid to countries that had been badly affected by the Second World War.

Nation of Islam A group founded in 1931, which aimed to provide black Americans with an alternative to Christianity and to keep blacks and whites separate. It did not teach the orthodox Islamic faith.

Militant Aggressive in the support of a cause.

New Frontier Term used by John F. Kennedy to describe the challenges the US faced in the early 1960s.

Red Scare Term used in the USA after the communist revolution in Russia in 1917. It was the fear that immigrants from Eastern Europe would bring to the USA ideas about a communist revolution.

Republican Supporter of the Republican Party, whose main ideas were to keep taxes low, limit the powers of the federal government, follow policies that favoured business and encourage self-sufficiency.

Segregation Separating groups due to their race or religion. This could include separate housing, education, health treatment, access to public buildings.

Segregationists Those who believed in the policy of separation of races.

Senate The Upper House of the US Congress (parliament).

Senator Member of the Senate. There are two senators per state.

Separatism Keeping races apart.

Sexual permissiveness Freedom to have relationships outside marriage, often with more than one partner.

Sit-in A form of civil disobedience in which demonstrators occupy a public place and, as a protest, refuse to move.

Student Non-violent Co-ordinating Committee (SNCC) Founded by students at Shaw University, North Carolina. Its aim was to attack examples of discrimination and by peaceful methods demand equality for black Americans.

Superpowers At the end of the war, the USA and USSR were so powerful in military and economic terms that they had left all other countries behind.

Supreme Court The highest federal court in the USA, consisting of nine judges chosen by the president, who make sure that the president and Congress obey the rules of the Constitution.

Truman Doctrine A statement by the US President Truman in 1947 promising support for any countries threatened with a communist revolution.

United Nations International organisation set up at the end of the Second World War to maintain world peace.

USSR Name given to Russia after the Bolshevik Revolution.

Vietnam War Attempt by communist North Vietnam to take over South Vietnam.

White Citizens' Councils Groups of white people who worked to maintain segregation.

White supremacists People who believed that white people were superior to black people.

Youth culture Beliefs, attitudes and interests of teenagers.

Index